SHORTNESS

A KEY TO BETTER BIDDING

JAMES MARSH STERNBERG MD (DR J)

authorHOUSE

AuthorHouse™
1663 Liberty Drive
Bloomington, IN 47403
www.authorhouse.com
Phone: 833-262-8899

Published by AuthorHouse 11/24/2021

ISBN: 978-1-6655-4568-6 (sc)
ISBN: 978-1-6655-4567-9 (e)

CONTENTS

DEDICATION

In Memory Of

MARSHA
STERNBERG

They were all for you

Never Forgotten

Also By James Marsh Sternberg

Playing To Trick One, No Mulligans in Bridge

Trump Suit Headaches, Rx for Declarers

The Finesse, Only a Last Resort

Blocking and Unblocking

Shortness – A Key to Better Bridge

When Michaels Meets the Unusual

With Danny Kleinman

Second Hand High, Third Hand Not Too High

An Entry, An Entry, My Kingdom For An Entry

L O L, Loser – On – Loser

The Search for a Second Suit

ACKNOWLEDGEMENTS

This book would not have been possible without the help of several friends. Frank Stewart, Michael Lawrence, Anne Lund, Eddie Kantar, and Marty Bergen all provided suggestions for material for the book.

I am forever indebted to Hall of Famer Fred Hamilton and the late Bernie Chazen and Allen Cokin, without whose guidance and teaching I could not have achieved whatever success I have had in bridge.

I want to thank my editor Danny Kleinman for his valuable assistance.

Any errors in the books are totally mine.

And of course Vickie Lee Bader, whose love and patience helped guide me thru the many hours of this endeavor.

James Marsh Sternberg, MD

Palm Beach Gardens, FL

mmay001@aol.com

INTRODUCTION

This book is about only one topic. Shortness, singletons and voids. It's impossible to overestimate the value distribution plays in bidding accuracy. High cards are nice; anybody can bid games and slams when the high cards are falling out of their hands onto the table.

But those results don't get you very far. It's an average or maybe just above. You don't win bridge tournaments that way. The pairs who bid games and slams on fewer HCP and who accurately stay out of bad games and slams, those are the winners. When the 'room' is in 3NT scoring +460 or +490 and you are in six diamonds scoring +920, then come and tell me about it.

I've tried to show different ways a player can ask or tell about shortness. The book is divided into chapter on offense and defense. Some chapters are very short. Some chapters have example deals at the end of the chapter. The major chapter focuses on splinter bidding with many example hands.

While this is a book about bidding, for completeness, the last three chapters focus on card play, defending with and against singletons. Besides, I thought I needed to make the book a bit longer so you would feel you got your money's worth.

There are lots of different ways to do things in bridge. I've presented some systems I've learned over the years from some of the best. This is one way and you may prefer something else. Whatever works, great.

I want to give you some things to think about and suggest solutions.

I hope you find it helpful at the table.

James Marsh Sternberg, MD
Palm Beach Gardens, FL
mmay001@aol.com

Counting Shortness

Charles Goren, in his original literature, suggested that besides the 4321 for honors, add three points for a void, two points for a singleton, and one point for a doubleton. Don't get my good friend and expert player and writer Jerry Helms started on this topic. Quoting Jerry from one of his terrific "Ask Jerry" columns, "I respectfully but vehemently disagree!" As an example, Jerry showed this hand ♠A873 ♡ void ♢AK862 ♣QJ75 and asked that if the contract were in any number of hearts or notrump, would you proudly table this dummy proclaiming your seventeen points?

No, of course not. As opener or responder, we count our HCP and length points in our initial evaluation of our hand. Long suits are usually an asset in any contract. After a major suit fit has been found, shortness in the dummy is a useful asset. This may or may not necessarily be the opening bidder.

A question always asked is how many tricks do you have with spades as trump?

DECLARER	DUMMY
♠ A K Q J 10	♠ 9 8 7
♡ 5	♡ 4 3 2

The answer is exactly five. If the ♡Ace is led followed by more hearts, declarer can ruff to prevent a loser, but cannot create an extra winner. His shortness is useless. In fact, it's a potential liability, because each heart play is shortening his trump holding.

However, with shortness in the dummy:

DECLARER	DUMMY
♠ A K Q J 10	♠ 9 8 7
♡ 5 4 3	♡ 2

On this layout with shortness in dummy, seven tricks are available, or six if the opponents lead trumps, since by ruffing in the short hand, winners are created.

Eddie Kantar said "unless you are the seventh son of a seventh son, you can't tell whether your short suits will be worth anything until you hear the bidding."

If you have four-card support for responder, now be greedy and re-evaluate. Add a point for a doubleton, three for a singleton, and five for a void.

Consider this hand. How would you "count" it?

♠ 3 ♡ K Q 5 4 ♦ A 10 5 2 ♣ K J 6 5

An opening hand, thirteen HCP but after 1♦ – 1♠, you have a minimum and already have a rebid problem, a topic we will discuss in a later chapter.

But if partner responds 1♡, now what? 2♡? Something else?

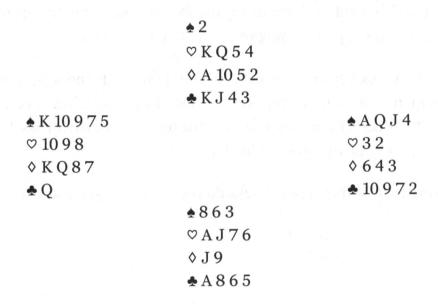

If you bid 2♡, South would pass. West led the ♠ 10.

East won Trick 1 and returned a trump. Declarer won the ♡J and ruffed a spade with dummy's other low trump. She returned to her hand with the ♣A and ruffed her last spade with ♡Q. She cashed the ♡K and the ♦A. Then she gave up a diamond. West won and continued spades. Declarer ruffed with the ♡7, drew the last trump and conceded a club at the end. An easy ten tricks.

Asses the blame if you didn't get to four hearts. Who was at fault?

100% to North, the point counter. Yes, still thirteen HCP in high cards, but as dummy, now the singleton is huge. The hand is certainly worth a raise to 3♡ and of course South would bid game.

Another question often asked is which is better: playing in a 5-3 or a 4-4 trump fit when you have a double fit. Yes, some of my students tell me they prefer the 5-3 because they feel better having 'more' trumps; it's cozier. Well, that's nice I tell them, but I also tell them they are not here to feel good.

The reason a 4-4 is usually better than a 5-3 is that with a 4-4, either hand may become the 'short' hand to create extra tricks by ruffing, while at the same time, the 5-3 may serve as a second suit to discard losers. (Yes, a dummy reversal is an exception).

For example:

♠ Q J 4
♡ Q J 10 8
♢ A 6 3
♣ A Q 2

♠ A K 10 9 7
♡ A K 9 7
♢ 8 7 5
♣ 3

With spades as trump, there are eleven tricks: five spades, four hearts, one diamond, and one club. The only possibility for another trick is a club finesse which never works in my books.

With hearts as trump, however, you take six trump tricks including two club ruffs in the short hand, five spades and two aces for thirteen winners with any reasonable breaks.

Asking and Telling

Having I hope convinced you of the importance of shortness, let's talk briefly about asking and telling. Bridge systems can get very complex. Sometimes too much memory is involved and if that is the case, then whatever you are playing is not worth it. If one partner forgets something, you obviously were better off playing simple 'mama-papa' and avoiding accidents. By keeping consistency in your system, you can try to avoid memory problems.

In the coming chapters, we are going to cover a lot. So lets try to make it simple. A player is going to be either asking or telling about shortness.

If he is 'telling', he is naming his suit. A simple example:
1♠ - 2NT, a Jacoby Forcing Raise, a common convention
3◇- I have a singleton or void in diamonds. Notice he is telling, not asking.
A natural bid, easy.

Let's talk about 'asking'. This is where different systems vary, where memory will drive you crazy. I like to keep it simple, no memory. Bridge systems need to be logical. The more there is to memorize, the more there is to forget. It's very simple, everyone forgets. Let me suggest this to you. But I want to warn you in advance:
1) This is not the way everyone plays, and 2) not necessarily the way someone else may tell you. Just think about it and decide what you like.

Whenever partner asks you a question, the next bid says NO. Think about it this way. You play Stayman, right. So 1NT – 2♣. Do you have a 4-card major?
What do you do when you do not? Yes, you make the next bid- 2◇, NO, I do NOT have a 4-card major.

So do the same anytime you are asked a question. First step is NO. Suppose after a 4NT bid, you responded 5♣, whatever that means in your system. And I bid 5◇ asking if you have the trump queen. What's the way to say NO? 5♡, the first step. Let me repeat. This is not standard. But it's easier, logical, and nothing to forget. The first step is always no.

Another example: You open 2♠ and we are playing after Weak Two bids, that 2NT asks if you have a singleton. How do you say NO? 3♣! First step. OK, Jim you ask, how do I show my singleton? Easy, it's always up-the-line. NEVER memorize anything! There are three possible singletons. ♣, ◊, ♡. Lowest, or middle, or highest.

So if you have a singleton, the positive answers are 3◊, 3♡, 3♠, showing in order, a singleton ♣, ◊, or ♡, just up-the-line. NO memory.

We will see this many times as we go thru the book. Low, middle, high.
** Yes, many players prefer going back to the trump suit as the "no" response, naming the suits, etc. Your choice but I prefer to keep it the same throughout.

Another example might help. You are playing that after 1♡-2♡, or 1♠-2♠, opener can ask responder if he has a singleton.

Let's use 1♡-2♡. So 2♠, the next bid is the ask.
> 2NT = NO
> 3♣ - singleton club. Here the responses happen to fall on the suit
> 3◊ - singleton diamond
> 3♡ - single SPADE (logical, 2NT was NO)

1♠ - 2♠
2NT asks
> 3♣ =NO
> 3◊ - singleton club (Lowest)
> 3♡ - singleton diamond (Middle)
> 3♠ - singleton heart (Highest)

Imagine trying to memorize all this is asking for a migraine. They would come and lock you up. Notice this way there is nothing to memorize; it's always NO, the lower, middle, higher. It NEVER varies so there is nothing to think about. Most teachers (and your partner) are probably trying to give you a migraine.

Shortness: The Good and the Bad

Expert bidders have realized for a long time, since the days of Charles Goren, that one of the most important keys to successful bidding lies in the ability for one or both partners to be able to tell the other about shortness in his or her hand. At other times, one partner may act based on his own shortness. This is especially important in two situations.

The first is in reaching games or slams with less than the usual number of high card points. Being able to recognize the lack of wasted values, the so-called '30 or 34 point deck' where one partner has a low singleton and the partner's holding is on the order of three or four small, x facing xxxx. When one partner is void, it's a "30 point deck." In these instances, instead of the usual 26 and 33 points which are the usual benchmarks for games and small slams, these can be bid with considerable fewer values.

After all, when one player opens a 15-17 point notrump and his partner has 18+ points, you can expect everyone is going to bid a small slam for an average result. Winning comes from bidding slams with 26-28 HCP's. That's usually a top board.

The other important situation is recognizing shortness to stay out of 3NT when it is wrong. For example, to recognize your partner has Jxx of a suit and you have a singleton. If we find a major suit fit, it's usually not a problem. But if not, and we have enough high cards for game, we are thinking about 3NT rather than five or six of a minor.

How often has your partner opened 1NT and you have ten to twelve HCP, but your distribution is 3=1=4=5 or 1=3=5=4? Of course, you raise to 3NT and partner has Jxx opposite your singleton. It's very annoying to watch the opponents take the first five tricks.

The best partnerships have their systems geared to be able to focus on showing shortness before committing to 3NT with this thought in mind. "If I know that my partner knows I have a singleton____(whatever), and he still wants to be in 3NT,

I feel a lot better. After all, she might have something like AQJ or the likes."

This is important not only after NT openings, but also after minor suit raises, regular or inverted and 1 minor – 2NT auctions. We will explore all these issues in the coming chapters.

Splinters: All Sizes and Shapes

What is a splinter? Sure, a sliver of wood stuck under your skin that hurts.

But in bridge, it's a convention, the use of a jump to show a particular short suit with length in partner's suit, necessary to be able to ruff the short suit.

The concept was developed independently by David Cliff in 1963 who was the first to publish an article on the subject, and by Dorothy Hayden Truscott in the early sixties which she described in the first edition of her book "Bid Better, Play Better," under the heading of The Unusual Jump to Show a Singleton. Even the famous expert BJ Becker, a notoriously natural bidder in those early days, immediately saw the benefits and adopted this radical artificial convention. It's come a long way since.

One benefit is obvious. The bids that are commonly used as splinters are otherwise of little use as natural bids. Can you think of a hand with which you would want to bid 4◊ as a natural bid after partner opened 1♡? I don't think so. In a competitive situation, it's a different story as we might want to preempt. After 1♡ - double or an overcall, we might want to bid 4◊ as a natural preempt to shut out your left hand opponent.

In this book, I'm going to show you many (maybe too many?) ways to show shortness, but splinter bidding is the most common convention. Anybody will bid game with 26 – 28 points, and slam with 33 – 35. But all that gets you is average. Reaching contracts with fewer points or avoiding bad games and slams when there is a duplication of values is what wins bridge tournaments.

This is where splinters, and other methods of finding shortness are so valuable. Having a method to explore to find these hands is generally not available using purely natural bids.

Splinter bids show extra values since they force the bidding a level higher. How much extra depends on the auction as we will see.

One word of caution. You don't want to have accidents in the bidding. Splinters come in all shapes and sizes. To what degree you and your partner treat some bids as splinters may vary.

Try to never make a splinter bid unless you are 100% positive that your partner will understand the bid. Every partnership must do some homework before using any splinters.

You need discuss a partnership philosophy and write down your agreements. Anything from basic conservative to the extreme 'I never met a splinter I didn't like' is fine as long as you are both on the same wavelength. Otherwise, the number of accidents will require keeping a liability lawyer on retainer.

Let's start with some basic examples and then move on. If the beginning seems too basic, bear with me. I'm sure I will pique your interest as we go on.

First a few important principles of bidding. How much information do you want to reveal to the opponents? They are probably listening. The more you squeal on your hand, the easier it will be for them to find a better opening lead to help them defend. Someone once said, "There are no bad opening leaders, only deaf ones."

When the limit of the deal is game, try to bid as uninformatively as possible. Try to get to game giving as little information as possible. For example, the Jacoby Forcing Raise convention as usually played, forces opener, the closed hand, to disclose his singleton at his second call even though responder may have no slam interest.

There are better ways to handle this, which we will discuss in subsequent chapters. On the other hand, a convention like the so-called 'Spiral', only reveals information about what will be in the dummy.

If the partnership is in the slam zone, the cost of revealing information will be compensated by better slam bidding. The significance of this in splinter bidding will become evident as we proceed.

Besides the above, consider these two important guiding principles.

1) One player must limit his values to allow the other to judge the level the partnership should seek, partial, game, or slam.
2) One player must describe his shape to allow the other to determine whether his high cards are working. In this regard, note there are two ways to help partner tell which high cards are working and which are idle. You can bid a suit, a fragment bid, to tell him face cards in that suit are working, or show shortness to tell him face cards in that suit are idle.

Let me show you some examples:

Auction # 1	1♠ - 2♠	They have stopped in game while revealing a
	3◊ - 4♣	lot of information. Did anyone really have any
	4♠ - P	slam ambitions?

| Auction # 2 | 1♠ - 2 minor, game forcing | |
| | 2♠ - 3♠ | Neither hand is limited. Without good further methods, slam exploration will be awkward to help limit one of these hands. |

| Auction # 3 | 1 minor – 1 Major | |
| | 4 of that Major | Neither partner has described his shape. They will have a hard time judging when their high cards are or are not working. |

THE MOST COMMON: Here is the one I'm sure most of you already play.

1♠ - 4♣, 4◊, 4♡ - Singletons or voids, anchoring spades as trumps.

1♡ - 3♠, 4♣, 4◊ - Same

What's the purpose of the splinter? Not to hear yourself talk, or just because you have a new toy to use. Opposite a 1♠ opening bid, this hand would be a fine 4◊ splinter: ♠ K 7 6 3   ♡ A 9 3   ◊ 4   ♣ K J 8 6 4

If partner held: ♠ A Q 9 5 2   ♡ K Q 7   ◊ 8 7 3   ♣ A 9
you would reach an excellent 6♠ on only 26 HCP.

But give partner: ♠ K Q 10 8 2   ♡ K 8 6   ◊ K 10   ♣ A 10 2
with diamond wastage, the same 26 HCP, game is the limit of the deal.

4-level splinter bids like the above should be limited to around 13-15+ dummy support points. You have a 4-level bid, no more and are prepared to pass partner's decision to stop. With a stronger hand, you must find a different auction, either starting with a Jacoby Forcing Raise or a game forcing 2/1 bid.

4-level splinters suggest slams, nor necessarily on the basis of points, but on fits and distribution. An invitational looking hand when you first pick it up like:

♠ Q J 7 5 3   ♡ A 6 4   ◊ A 10 6 4   ♣ 7

is certainly suddenly worth a 4♣ slam try splinter when partner opens 1♠.

Had partner opened 1♣ and rebid 1NT, even game might be questionable.

I believe when one makes a 4-level splinter over 1 Major opening, ideally responder should have a control, an ace or king in both of the other two suits.

For example if partner opened 1♠, and I held:

♠ A Q 7 4 2   ♡ 5   ◊ 5 3 2   ♣ A K J 7

I would prefer to use 2NT as an artificial forcing spade raise rather than bid 4♡, a splinter with three small diamonds. Partner has no room to move. He has to sign-off or go past game. Just because you have a toy doesn't mean you have to play with it. Some say 2NT must be balanced. Others say if unbalanced, implies a weak fragment such as in the hand above or the lack of a good 5-card suit.

Let's look at three more and see what to do:

1)	♠ A 7 6 4	♡ Q J 5 3	◊ J 10 5 3	♣ 6
2)	♠ A 8 6 4	♡ Q J 6 4	◊ K 10 6 4	♣ 8
3)	♠ A K Q 5	♡ A Q 6 4	◊ Q 10 7 4	♣ 8

Hand # 1 is only worth a limit raise. Nice shape, nice trump, but a little skinny in strength. Partner will expect more.

Hand # 2 is perfect for a 4♣ splinter. Right on shape, right on strength, and happy to accept partner's decision.

Hand # 3 is too strong. The problem is if partner signs off in game, you will want to make one more try. Is the 5-level safe? 4-level splinters should be 4-level bids, no more, no less. The diamond suit lacks a control. Start with your non splinter game forcing raise to leave more room.

Partner could have ♠ J10972 ♡ KJ2 ◊ A3 ♣ 975, a laydown slam.

HOW SHOULD OPENER CONTINUE?

OK, now what? You have opened the bidding with one of a major and partner has made a 4-level splinter, a slam try. To consider slam you need a hand with at least thirteen high cards in our new 34-point deck, 30 for 10 in each of the three other suits and 4 for the ace in the splinter suit. If partner has a void, it's a 30-point deck.

Now recount your high cards, excluding the king, queen, and jack in the splintered suit. Still interested? Good, now another important consideration is having controls; aces, kings, and maybe shortness of your own. You don't want the opponents to take the first two tricks or be able to make a lead to set up the setting trick once they take their ace. Is your AQx in the splinter suit a vital control or window dressing? Big difference opposite a singleton compared to opposite a void.

You will recall I suggested partner have side suit controls himself. Another consideration is trump suit quality. Yes, you both can't have the AKQ but you might be needing to use dummy's good trumps for ruffing. Having your good trumps to draw trumps later is a big plus. And you don't want to lose both that outside ace and a trump trick.

	North		North		North
4)	♠ 9 5 4	5)	♠ K Q 7 5 2	6)	♠ K Q 7 5 2
	♡ A K 7 5 3 2		♡ A 7 4		♡ K Q 10 5
	◊ K Q 4		◊ K Q 10 5		◊ A 7 4
	♣ 7		♣ 7		♣ 7

South	South	South
♠ A J 7 3	♠ J 9 8 3	♠ J 9 8 3
♡ Q 9 8 6	♡ 9	♡ 9
◊ 8	◊ A 4 2	◊ A 3 2
♣ A J 6 2	♣ A K J 6 2	♣ A K J 6 2

4) 1♡ - 4◊ - 4♡. North's diamond suit carries wasted values, making the hand worth much lass, no chance for slam.

5) 1♠ - 4♡ - 4NT – 5♡ - 6♠ The ace of hearts is not wasted. The two small hearts can be ruffed. A good slam.

6) 1♠ - 4♡ - 4♠ As with (4), too much wastage. Interchange the hearts with one of the minors, now you have something.

DELAYED RESPONDER SPLINTERS:

Once the trump suit has been agreed upon, jump bids in unbid suits are almost always splinters. For example:

1) South: ♠6 ♡A Q 4 3 ◊K Q 4 ♣A 10 9 7 5

North	South
1♣	1♡
2♡	3♠

Yes, partner only made a single raise showing 12-14. But he certainly could have the right hand for slam; you have a double fit. As long as his values are not wasted in spades, slam is possible.

But if you just raise to 4♡, that's the end of the auction. If you bid 3♠, at least he will know you read this book.

2) North: ♠K Q 5 ♡A K 8 6 4 2 ◊5 ♣9 7 5

North	South
1♡	2◊* * Game forcing
2♡	3♡

Wouldn't we all just bid 4♡?

South's possible hands: a) ♠A J 6   ♡Q 9 5   ◊A J 7 6 2   ♣Q 2
                              b) ♠A 8 6 4 ♡Q 9 5   ◊A J 7 6 2   ♣2

Notice with hand (a), the limit of the deal is game, 26 HCP.

Notice with hand (b), which should have bid 4♣, a cold slam, 23 HCP.

OPENER CAN SPLINTER TOO: A TYPICAL EXAMPLE

Opener	Responder	WEST	EAST	
♠ K Q 6 3	♠ A 9 8 7	1♣	1♠	
♡ A Q 9	♡ K 8 7	4◊*	4NT	* Splinter Spade Raise
◊ 7	◊ 8 6 4 2	5◊^	5♡*	^ 0 or 3 * Queen ask
♣ A Q J 10 9	♣ K 3	6♠^	P	^ Yes, no kings,
				1ˢᵗ step, 5♠= No

Notice how if West had simply raised 1♠ to 4♠, East would have no idea if he should go on. Looking at four small diamonds, he would probably pass. I would.

Opener can self-splinter: ♠ A K J 10 9 7 5 ♡ K J 10 ◊ K 6 ♣ 3

While some might incorrectly open 2♣, I would open 1♠. If as so often, partner bids 1NT, forcing or whatever, rebid 4♣. This can't be clubs since 3♣ would be a strong jump shift. 4♣ is a 4♠ bid with a singleton club. Let's see what partner has to say.

Responder can also self-splinter after being raised. In this case, the player making the splinter bid initiated the trump suit himself. Here is an example:

♠ A Q 8 6 4 2   ♡ K J 6   ◊ 7   ♣ A 9 7

1♣   1♠

2♠   ? Slam is certainly possible depending on the location of partner's values. The best way to describe your hand is to 'tell', bid 4◊ and let partner look at her hand (hopefully).

Partner's hand: ♠ K 7 5 3   ♡ A 4   ◊ 6 4 2   ♣ K Q 8 6
With this hand, partner should bid 4NT and reach 6♠.

But just reverse the minors to this position:
You: ◊ 7   ♣ A 9 7

Partner: ◊ K Q 8 6   ♣ 6 4 2

Same shape, same HCP, but game is high enough.

SELF SPLINTER AFTER 1 MINOR - 1NT RESPONSE

Here is an auction that might leave partner unsure of how to proceed:

1 minor -   1NT
3 Major   Is this jump reverse by opener a self splinter?
            Yes. A reverse is unlimited; there are no 'Super reverses'.
So this unnecessary jump qualifies as a splinter. Opener has a hand like:

♠2 ♡A64 ◇AKJ864 ♣AQ8

On this auction, responder rates to have a number of clubs. The right contract could be 3NT, 5 or 6♣, or 5 or 6◇.

SPLINTERS WITH SINGLE JUMPS:

We will cover this in detail in following chapters but here are several examples:

# 1		# 2		# 3	
North	South	North	South	North	South
1♠	2♣	1NT	2♡ (Transfer)	1♡	2♡
2♠	4◇*	2♠	4♣* or 4◇*	4♣* or 4◇*	

*All bids marked with (*) are splinter bids, showing shortness in the agreed suit. Why? In # 1 because 3◇ would be natural and forcing. In # 2, three of a minor would be natural and game forcing, and in # 3, three of a minor would be forcing, some type of game try.

A SPLINTER IN OPENER'S SECOND SUIT:

It's very logical. Simply because it's a double jump to four of a minor on the second round. On the first round, it would be a natural bid. For example:

North South South's hand: ♠AK64 ♡AQ86 ◇QJ85 ♣5
1♣   1♡
1♠   4♣   If South rebid 2♣, that would be weak, a sign-off. If South bid 3♣, that's invitational. To force in clubs and not go past 3NT, a possible contract on a different hand, South would bid 3◇, 4th suit artificial and game forcing. So 4♣ can't be clubs.
            Rather it's a splinter raise of North's last bid suit, spades.

MINI - SPLINTERS

So far we have been discussing mostly slammish splinters. But splinters come in all sizes. Marty Bergen coined the term "splimit", a fancy term for a limited splinter. But these are very useful in many ways. Let's start with the smallest.

The auction starts: 1 minor -1 Major - 3 Same Major.

South North

1♣   1♠

3♠   What does that mean? South has four spades and in support of spades 15-17 points. Non-forcing, invitational, and North has to decide should she go on.

She could have either:

♠ K Q 8 5 3	♠ K Q 8 5 3
♡ Q 7	♡ 8 7 4 3
◊ 8 7 4 3	◊ Q 7
♣ 9 6	♣ 9 6

It's a close decision; pass or go on. Either could be right. What will matter is how the hands fit. Let's see how partner might have made it easier for you.

1♣   1♠

3◊ (or 3♡)   What do those bids mean? Diamonds? Hearts? What happened to bidding at the two level, 2◊ or 2♡? Yes, those bids would be reverses showing big hands. Are 3◊/3♡ super reverses?
Nonsense, no such thing. These 3-bids are splinters, a raise to 3♠ with shortness in the suit bid. Which bid do you think will be more helpful to North in deciding whether or not to bid 4♠? A simple raise to 3♠ or a descriptive 3◊ splinter raise?

Openers hand: ♠ A 10 9 4   ♡ K 6 2   ◊ 9   ♣ A K J 4 3.

You can only mini-splinter up, on these four auctions:

1♣ - 1♠; 3◊   1♣ - 1♠; 3♡
1♣ - 1♡; 3◊   1◊ - 1♠; 3♡

1◊ - 1 Major – 3♣, jumping 'down', is a natural strong jump shift. Yes, 4♣ is a splinter, but that's a game force, slam invite. In making a go or no-go game determination, or higher, after a mini, responder uses the same criteria we have been discussing, ie: what am I holding in partner's short suit.

UNTANGLING YOUR MAJOR SPLINTERS

An additional and final (yea sure, you say) thought on the majors.
The mini-splinter has another important use.

You hold: ♠ A Q 3 2   ♡ A Q 4   ◊ 9   ♣ A K Q 9 4

You correctly open 1♣ instead of an awkward 2♣ and partner bids 1♠. You bid 4◊, and partner bids 4♠. Are you done? Of course not. You want to go at least once more. 4NT? Are you safe at the five level?

Here is an easy solution for these occasional 5-level hands. Mini-splinter. Bid only 3◊. (If partner passes, call me and I'll find you a new partner for next week). But let's say partner is awake. If partner signs off in 3♠, you bid 4♠. Partner should wonder, if you were always going to 4♠, why didn't you splinter with 4◊?

Because you were too strong. Now partner knows you have a five bid and should go on with almost anything; ♠ Kxxxx and another good card is a slam.

And if over your mini-splinter, partner bids 4♠ himself, you know you can go on. The other plus is that when you do make a 4-level splinter, partner knows you have a 'four and no more hand'.

Mini's occur about 95% of the time, but when the big one comes along, you will be ready. There is nothing worse than ending up at the five level, down one.

OK, so much for the majors. Let's move on.

More Splinter Bids After Minor Suit Openings

I'm going to cover this in great detail in a subsequent chapter on minor suit singleton bidding, but let's look at some general principles.

Similar rules apply when partner opens a minor, but much depends on your system. What does a 1♣ or 1♢ promise lengthwise? If both show at least three and 1♢ is almost always four, splinters can still be used but more care must be exercised.

Your hand: ♠ A J 3   ♡ 5   ♢ K Q 10 6 4   ♣ K 10 6 4   Partner opens 1♢.

Depending on your system, you can make an inverted forcing raise first. If not, you can start with a 2♣ response. To reach the best contract, describe your hand with a splinter raise, 3♡, game forcing with heart shortness and diamond length.

How should opener respond? Here are three possible opening hands.

	1)	2)	3)
	♠ K Q 2	♠ K 9 2	♠ K Q 9 2
	♡ 9 6 4 3	♡ K Q 10 7	♡ A 7 3
	♢ A J 8 3	♢ A 8 5 3	♢ J 8 5 3
	♣ A 3	♣ 9 3	♣ Q 3

Responder's Hand (repeated for convenience):

♠ A J 3   ♡ 5   ♢ K Q 10 6 4   ♣ K 10 6 4

Hand # 1, only a balanced 14-count has slam possibilities for sure. Knowing partner has a singleton heart means a 34 point deck. The black suit honors rate to all be working opposite partner's length. Whatever system you have to ask for Keycards is next.

Hand # 2, your heart values rate to be useless in a high diamond contract. But in 3NT, they are worth at least two or more tricks. Bid 3NT. It's "partner knows that you know."

Hand #3, with only one heart stopper, to make 3NT after a heart lead, you will probably need to take the first nine tricks. Five diamonds is likely to be a better contract despite your weak trump. Both partners can't have the AKQ.

Let's look at two more opening hands after 1♦ - 3♡.

4) ♠ A J 5   5) ♠ A J 5
    ♡ K Q 10   ♡ K 7 3
    ◇ K 6 4 3   ◇ K Q 6 4
    ♣ K Q 3   ♣ K Q 10

Responder's Hand: ♠ K 7 6   ♡ 9   ◇ A J 7 5 2   ♣ A J 8 6

Hand # 4, opener's honor values in the splinter suit are not ruffable, but are useful for taking tricks in a notrump contract.

Hand # 5, is more suitable for a possible diamond slam. Without the necessary aces in opener's hand, 5♦ would be the limit of the deal.

SPLINTERS IN SUPPORT OF RESPONDER'S MINOR

This topic can be played in two ways, but the most popular way among expert partnerships is the following.

North South
1♠   2♣
3◇   Is it diamonds with extras or is it a splinter for clubs? There are two schools of thought, but most play this as a splinter, following the general principle of an unnecessary jump in a new suit is a splinter.

As dealer you opener 1♠ with   ♠ A K 8 6 4   ♡ K 9 7   ◇ 3   ♣ K Q 8 7

After partner responds 2♣, what is the best description of your hand?

Now what? Let's look at three hands responder might hold.

1) ♠ J 3   2) ♠ Q 3   3) ♠ J 3
    ♡ Q J 5 2   ♡ A 8 4   ♡ Q 10 2
    ◇ A 8 4   ◇ J 8 4   ◇ A Q J
    ♣ A J 6 3   ♣ A J 9 5 3   ♣ J 10 9 3 2

Hand # 1, partner will realize 3NT will be in danger with a diamond lead, again needing the first nine tricks. A 5-2 spade contract would be subjected to repeated diamond plays, shortening declarer's trumps. Five clubs rates to be a good contract.

Hand # 2, partner will recognize the slam potential. Only 27 HCP but a 34 point deck makes six clubs an odds-on favorite.

Hand # 3, is the opposite. With so much strength in the diamond suit facing shortage, certainly 3NT is the contract of choice.

WHAT ABOUT AFTER PARTNER OVERCALLS?

North PARTNER South

1♣   1♠   If South passes, bids 1NT, 2 ♣, 2◊, or (2♡),

West (You)
a jump bid by you to
4♣ or 4◊ would be a
splinter spade raise.
4♡ would be to play.
Except after 2♡

SPLINTERING WITH AN HONOR

What, are you trying to start an argument? It depends who you ask. And I'm not naming names. There is really no argument about singleton queens and jacks, just treat them as singletons. But what about aces and kings?

I know some of the top players in the world who have no hesitation about splintering with an ace if that's what seems to be the best description of the hand.

I know others who wouldn't do it if you put a gun against their head. Kings are even worse. This hand was recently submitted to a writer in the Bulletin for comment:

♠ K J 10 9 5 4 3   ♡ J 5 2   ◇ A   ♣ K 6

Her partner opened 1NT, 15-17. She transferred to 2♠, then bid 4◇, a splinter. She hoped partner could cue bid 4♡. Her partner bid 4♠ ending the auction with:

♠ Q 6   ♡ A K 10 3   ◇ Q 8 4   ♣ A J 7 4 and of course placed the blame on responder muttering some nonsense about responder should have bid Blackwood, the usual 'cure-all'.

Expert Billy Miller pointed out responder had bid perfectly, first showing length in one suit, then shortness in another suit. At that point, Billy wrote, opener was invited to sign off, make a counter slam try, or bid Keycard herself. He wrote "Personally I do not have any problem making a splinter bid with a singleton ace, although I do know some experts who hate it."

When Marty Bergen was asked this question a few years ago, he wrote "Because many teachers and authors have been so vocal in advising against splintering with a singleton ace or king, and because I feel so strongly that their advice is impractical, I must reiterate: While splintering with a singleton honor is not perfect, neither are most bids. A splinter tells your partner a great deal of useful information about your hand. That's good enough for me." (ACBL Bulletin, June, 2014).

Me? Frankly, my dear, I don't give a damn, said someone years ago. If they can't decide, don't ask me. What do I know? I'm just a radiologist. I can only see thru the cards, not tell you what to do.

SPLINTERS WITH ONLY THREE TRUMPS

What, against the law? Infrequent but sometimes the best way to describe your hand. Mike Lawrence showed this hand and suggested the following auction.

As South, you hold   ♠ K 10 5   ♡ 3   ◇ K 9 7 3   ♣ A Q 8 7 3

North South

1♠   2♣

2♠   4♡ Since 3♡ would be forcing, 4♡ must be a splinter. If South had four spades, he might have either splintered or bid 2NT, an artificial game force on the first round.

What better way to describe this hand? As Mike pointed out, here are two possible hands for opener:

1)   ♠ Q J 9 7 6 2   ♡ K Q 8   ◇ Q J   ♣ K 3

                        or

2)   ♠ A Q J 8 4   ♡ 9 7 2   ◇ A 8 6   ♣ K 3

Both 14-point hands but what a difference. Hand #1 can make four spades while Hand #2 is certainly worth bidding six spades.

Another example is a hand Marty Bergen showed some years ago.

♠ A Q 8 6   ♡ K 7 3   ◇ 2   ♣ K Q 9 7 4

Partner opens 1♡ and the auction proceeds:

North   South

1♡   2♣

2♡   4◇   Since 3◇ would be natural and forcing, 4◇ must be a delayed splinter. Lacking four trumps, South bid clubs first, then the delayed 4◇ splinter told partner that you only held three-card support. Logically, the minimum strength needed for such bids is greater than with four trumps.

SPLINTERING WITH A VOID

While voids are very powerful especially when it comes to slam bidding, (I keep hearing Marty saying "I love voids"), splinters based on voids can be undesirable because partner will regard an ace holding, like Axx in that suit as an asset when it is practically useless.

You can splinter with a void if your hand is so strong you plan to follow with a 4NT Keycard ask after partner's sign-off. Note in such an auction, partner should disregard his ace in the splintered suit if he has it, a form of "Exclusion Blackwood". Why? If you had a Blackwood hand, why bother to splinter first?

AND IN COMPETITION?

1)

North	West	South	East
1♦	P	1♥	1♠
3♠			

A 4♥ bid with a singleton spade. 20 or so HCP and suggesting slam if South has the right hand.

But a good suggestion by Danny Kleinman, is to play a jump cue bid here is a void splinter and a simple cue bid as a singleton. If you want to raise hearts with a strong balanced hand, just raise to whatever level you feel your hand merits. Example:

2♠ - singleton 3♠ - void 4♥ - big balanced hand 2♥, 3♥ = raises

2) You are South holding ♠ A J 7 6 2   ♡ K 10 7   ◇ 6   ♣ A J 8 6

North	West	South	East
1♡	P	1♠	2♦
2♡	P	?	

A bid of 3♦ would be a general force, possible searching for 3NT. 4♥? Yes, you could just bid game, but you have good controls, good heart trump support, a singleton diamond, the list goes on. Can it hurt to bid 4♦ on the way? But a trump suit has not yet been agreed.

If North had something like: ♠ 5   ♡ A Q J 8 6 3   ◇ J 8 5 2   ♣ K Q she wasn't very excited when you bid 1♠. You are cold for 6♡ with 26 HCP.

Splinter bids in competition may not necessarily require more than game-going strength. With competitive bidding, it is important to describe your hand before a preemptive raise shuts out communication.

A lower bid in the splinter suit still must be forcing if the higher bid is to be recognized as a splinter. What does this mean?

South	West	North	East
1◊	1♡	1♠	2♡

4♣ - natural, because 3♣ is not forcing

South	West	North	East
1♣	P	1♠	2◊

3♡- normal jump shift (2♡ non forcing)

4◊ - splinter

4♡ - 5/6, natural

***In contested auctions, splinters only apply to the suit(s) bid by the opponents.

A splinter bid in an opposing suit is a single jump; a non-jump is a cue bid.

AFTER THE OPPONENTS OVERCALL

Marty Bergen asks an important question. Does your partnership treat responder's jump response in competition as a splinter or a preempt?

In his article, he cited this example from his own experience:

♠ K Q J 10 9 2   ♡ 8 4   ◊ 3   ♣ 10 9 5 2

His partner opened 1♡ and the next player overcalled 2◊. Marty bid 3♠, delighted to make a weak jump shift. He wanted to describe his hand and make life difficult for the opponents.

However, his partner bid Blackwood and drove to 6♡, thinking Marty had heart support and a singleton spade. You don't want to hear the 'rest of the story'.

Despite this one mishap, Marty believes in these competitive situations, these jumps should be natural and preemptive. Danny Kleinman also agrees than an auction such as 1♡ - Dbl – 4◊**(you)**, or 1♡ - simple overcall – 4◊**(you)**_ should be natural and preemptive.

Marty writes "while you are welcome to disagree.......more important to discuss with your partner(s) and....never have a similar disaster."

MISCELLANEOUS SPLINTERS

Concealed Splinters – You will occasionally play against, or may choose to play yourself concealed splinters. These are quite simple.

1♡ - 3♠ I have an undisclosed singleton or void somewhere

1♠ - 3♡ I have an undisclosed singleton or void somewhere

If partner has no slam interest, he signs off in game. If interested where responder's shortness is located, opener just makes the next bid, ie: 3♠/3♡ and 3NT/3♠. Shortness is shown up-the-line as previously discussed, low, middle, high.

These concealed splinters are easy and have value. An improvement is the ability to distinguish voids from singletons. To do this, responder makes a "strong jump shift" to show concealed shortness.

1♡ - 2♠, not 3, now there is room to show voids (Also called Bergen Splinters)

1♠ - 3♡ The first step still asks. All up-the-line responses

NO MEMORY

26

An example:

1♠ -	3♡ (I have undisclosed shortness, game forcing)
3♠ (where?)	3NT – I have a void

                                      4♣ - Where?

                                            Up the line, CDH

                                      4♣ - singleton club

                                      4♢ - singleton diamond

                                      4♡ - singleton heart

1♡	2♠ (I have undisclosed shortness, game forcing)
2NT (where?)	3♣ - I have a void

                                      3♢ - Where?

                                            Up the line, CDS

                                      3♢- singleton club (Lowest)

                                      3♡ - singleton diamond (Middle)

                                      3 ♠ - singleton spade (Highest)

The difference between singletons and voids cannot be overemphasized.

Let's look at one last simple way to differentiate these splinters.

VOIDS VERSUS SINGLETONS

A very good way to play is to distinguish immediately singletons from voids.

1♠ - 4♣, 4◊, 4♡ are singleton splinters

    3NT – I have a void splinter somewhere

        4♣ - Where?

            4◊, 4♡, 4♠ Up-the-line, LMH, ♣, ◊, ♡

1♡ - 3NT, 4♣, 4◊ are singleton splinters (some play 3NT=♠, others
                                up-the-line, LMH, ♣, ◊, ♠)

    3♠ I have a void splinter somewhere

        3NT – Where?

            4♣, 4◊, 4♡ - Up-the-line, LMH, ♣, ◊, ♠

JUST WHAT THE DOCTOR ORDERED

$$\spadesuit\ 8$$
$$\heartsuit\ K\,Q\,J\,9\,8\,6$$
$$\diamondsuit\ A\,Q$$
$$\clubsuit\ 9\,7\,4\,2$$

♠ K 7	♠ Q 10 5 3
♡ 7 2	♡ 3
◊ 10 9 4 3	◊ 8 7 6 5
♣ K J 10 8	♣ A Q 6 5

$$\spadesuit\ A\,J\,9\,6\,4$$
$$\heartsuit\ A\,10\,5\,4$$
$$\diamondsuit\ K\,J\,2$$
$$\clubsuit\ 3$$

South opened 1♠ and North bid 2♡, game forcing. South raised to 3♡ and North bid game. East led the ♠ 3.

Declarer won Trick 1 and drew trumps. He took twelve tricks, losing a club at the end. "Partner, were you looking at your hand during the bidding," asked North?

How should the auction have gone?

South	North	
1♠	2♡	South has a perfect hand to splinter in support of hearts.
4♣*	4NT	Four trump, a singleton club, nice controls. And of course,
5♡	6♡	North has just what the doctor ordered. Four small clubs opposite South's singleton.

Notice if North's minor suit holdings were reversed so they looked like this:

North: ◊ 9 7 4 2   ♣ A Q

South: ◊ K J 2   ♣ 3

How many losers might there be? Four hearts would certainly be high enough.

A TWO FOR ONE DEAL

          ♠ Q 6 3
          ♡ A K
          ♢ A Q 10
          ♣ 10 8 7 4 3

♠ A 5 2   ♠ 10 9 8 4
♡ Q 9 8 3 2   ♡ J 10 6 5 4
♢ 6 4 2   ♢ 9 8 5
♣ J 9   ♣ Q

          ♠ K J 7
          ♡ 7
          ♢ K J 7 3
          ♣ A K 6 5 2

North	South		South	North
1NT	3♡*		1♣	2♣^ ^ Forcing
3NT	4♣		3♡*	3NT
4♡	6♣		4♣	4♡
All Pass			6♣	All Pass
•	Splinter		*	Splinter

An interesting slam deal regardless of who deals.

With North as dealer opening 1NT, South splinters with 3♡, showing a 3=1=4=5 or 5=4 hand. North has hearts well stopped and bids 3NT. But when South shows extra values and bids his 5-card suit, North cue bids and South bids the slam.

With South as dealer, North bids 2♣ playing inverted minors and South shows his shortness. From there, the auction is similar to the other.

MINI-SPLINTER

```
                    ♠ Q 7 2
                    ♡ J 8 6 5 2
                    ◇ Q J 8
                    ♣ 9 2
  ♠ A J 5                              ♠ K 10 9 4
  ♡ 10                                 ♡ K 9 3
  ◇ K 10 7 5 4                         ◇ A 9 6 2
  ♣ 10 6 5 3                           ♣ Q 8
                    ♠ 8 6 3
                    ♡ A Q 7 4
                    ◇ 3
                    ♣ A K J 7 4
```

South	West	North	East
1♣	P	1♡	P
3♡		All Pass	

North had an easy pass over 3♡, having barely had his first bid. But what if he had a bit more?

How could South have made it easier for North?

South has the values for a raise to 3♡ but he should bid 3◇, a classic mini-splinter. North would be able to better evaluate his hand by looking at his diamond holding. "Do I have wasted values in diamonds," North would ask himself?

Since 2◇ would be a reverse, 3◇ is an unnecessary jump, hence a splinter. North is probably already too high in three hearts but that can't be helped.

COMPETITIVE BIDDING

North
♠ A 8 4 3
♡ 5
◇ Q 10 9 6 4
♣ A J 8

South	West	North	East
1♠	2♡	?	

Your call? 3◇? Some number of spades? Cue bid 3♡? Other?

What's it going to be? Decide before looking further.

3◇ would be game forcing, a 3/1 but would keep partner in the dark about the spade fit.

3♠? Much too good. You would bid 3♠ without the ace of spades so you can't make the same bid with the spade ace.

4♠? Pretty lazy and likely to end the auction.

3 ♡? Has merit. At least partner knows you have a good hand with spades.

And the winner is (drum roll please) 4♡, a splinter, singleton heart, four trump, some slam interest if partner is interested.

Partner's hand: ♠ K J 7 6 5 2   ♡ 8 3   ◇ A   ♣ K Q 6 3

Your splinter results in partner bidding 4NT, you bid 5♡, two keycards without the trump queen, and reach a nice 6♠.

HOW MANY?   3, 4, OR 5?

```
                      ♠ A 9 8 7 4 3
                      ♡ 6
                      ◊ J 10 9 7
                      ♣ Q J
        ♠ Q                                    ♠ 9 5
        ♡ 9 7 5 4                              ♡ Q 10 8 3
        ◊ Q 8 6 5                              ◊ A K 4 3
        ♣ 9 8 4 3                              ♣ 6 5 2
                      ♠ K J 10 2
                      ♡ A K J 2
                      ◊ 2
                      ♣ A K 10 7
```

South	West	North	East	
1♣	P	1♠	P	
4◊*	P	4♡^	P	* Splinter raise to the 4-level only ^ Cue bid
4NT	P	5♣	P	
5◊*	P	5♠^	P	* Do you have the trump Queen?
6♠		All Pass		^ Yes (Extra length compensates for the queen)
				First step, 5♡= No queen

South opened his nineteen HCP hand 1♣, hoping to hear either major. When North bid 1♠, South had a 4-level bid, no more, no less. A typical hand that will respect partner's decision to go or not go. If partner signed off with 4♠, South would not feel compelled to bid one more time.

Why not bid 3◊, a mini-splinter, then regardless, raise to 4♠?

That would be how South would bid with a 5-level bid, a hand like:

   ♠ A Q J 4   ♡ A K J   ◊ 8   ♣ A Q J 10 8

This 22 HCP hand needs little more than five spades to the king and a working card. If South bid that way with his nineteen count, then North, with:

   ♠ K 7 5 4 2   ♡ 9 7 3   ◊ 8 6 4 3   ♣ Q

would sign off over the 3◊ mini-splinter, but when South then bids 4♠, should carry on knowing partner has the 5-level drive. Have I completely confused you?

TIGER OR A WIMP

```
                        ♠ 2
                        ♡ A 10 9 6 4
                        ◇ A K J 6
                        ♣ A 6 2
    ♠ A K                                      ♠ Q J 10 8 5 3
    ♡ Q J 3 2                                  ♡ 7 5
    ◇ 2                                        ◇ 7 5
    ♣ Q J 10 9 8 7                             ♣ K 4 3
                        ♠ 9 7 6 4
                        ♡ K 8
                        ◇ Q 10 9 8 4 3
                        ♣ 5
```

West	North	East	South
1♣	1♡	1♠	P
2♣	2◇	2♠	3◇
	All Pass		

East led the ♠ Q and North quickly claimed twelve tricks.

"Really partner, you took your life in your hands and bid 3◇," said North.

"But I only had five HCP," lamented South.

As Mike Lawrence would say, "Yes, and a diamond is just a very old piece of coal." South was awarded the "Wimpy Bid of the Year" award.

What should South have bid?   4◇?   5◇?   Other?

In support of North, with six, count'em mister, as Bernie Chazen used to say, six pieces of trump and the king of partner's first suit, South's hand is a 'monster'.

How about a 4♣ splinter? Having previously passed, North won't expect more but will reach 6◇.

BROKE, BUT

```
              ♠ 8 7 4 2
              ♡ 10 8 3
              ◇ K 10 9 7 3
              ♣ 8
♠ 5 3                           ♠ J 6
♡ A J 9                         ♡ K 7 6 2
◇ Q 8                           ◇ J 6 5 4 2
♣ J 10 5 4 3 2                  ♣ 9 6
              ♠ A K Q 10 9
              ♡ Q 5 4
              ◇ A
              ♣ A K Q 7
```

South opened 2♣ and North bid 2◇, a waiting bid. South rebid 2♠, natural and forcing to at least 3♠. North jumped to 4♣. What's going on?

Well, I can tell you there is at least one person I play with who would think that was Gerber! I'm not kidding; all 4♣ bids for her are Gerber.

South of course knew better, since he had a rule with his partners. 4♣ is NEVER Gerber. I wholeheartedly subscribe to that rule, but that's a topic for another day.

South knew it was a splinter and cue bid 4◇. North bid 4♠ Now what would you do?

Well, if your partner could not cue bid a heart control, first or second round, and you are starring at ♡ Q 5 4, what do you think?

A prudent pass despite all those HCP is best. Do you agree with North's splinter with only three HCP?
I do; what if she had a singleton heart instead of a singleton club?
6♠ would be laydown.

AFTER A NEGATIVE DOUBLE

```
                    ♠ A Q 9 2
                    ♡ 10 6 3 2
                    ◊ Q 8
                    ♣ 7 6 2
      ♠ 10 3                              ♠ 7 6 5
      ♡ A K Q 8 5                         ♡ J 9 4
      ◊ J 9 6 4                           ◊ 5 3
      ♣ Q 9                               ♣ K J 10 8 5
                    ♠ K J 8 4
                    ♡ 7
                    ◊ A K 10 7 2
                    ♣ A 4 3
```

South	West	North	East
1◊	1♡	Dbl	P
3♡	P	4♠	All Pass

South opened 1◊. Had West passed and North had bid 1♠, what would you have rebid as South?

Probably a mini-splinter, 3♡, raising to 3♠ with a singleton heart. So what's changed? Nothing.

North looks at his heart holding, and visualizing a 34-point deck has no hesitation bidding 4♠.

A SLIGHT DELAY IS FINE

```
                        ♠ J 9 2
                        ♡ 2
                        ◊ A Q 7
                        ♣ A Q 8 4 3 2
      ♠ Q 10 3                              ♠ K 8 6 5 4
      ♡ A K 4                               ♡ Q J 10 5 3
      ◊ 6 4 3                               ◊ 5
      ♣ J 9 7 5                             ♣ 10 6
                        ♠ A 7
                        ♡ 9 8 7 6
                        ◊ K J 10 9 8 2
                        ♣ K
```

South	West	North	East	
1◊	P	2♣	P	
2◊	P	3♡*	P	* Splinter in support of diamonds
4◊*	P	5♣^	P	* Keycard ask in diamonds
6◊	All Pass			^ Two Keycards and the trump queen

South opened a hand marginal in HCP but with good trick taking potential. North bid 2♣, game forcing and when South rebid diamonds, made a splinter raise.

Visualizing exactly what he needed, South checked for Keycards. Notice that in the minor suits, the need to use a bid other than 4NT as the ask. The responses are too high.

A good slam on few HCP but lots of playing strength.

CHOICES

♠ A Q 8 5
♡ A 4
◊ 7
♣ A Q 10 8 7 6

♠ 3
♡ K Q 8 7 6
◊ Q 10 8 4 3
♣ 9 2

♠ 9 2
♡ J 10 9 5 3
◊ K J
♣ K J 4 3

♠ K J 10 7 6 4
♡ 2
◊ A 9 6 5 2
♣ 5

North	South
1♣	1♠
?	

North has several options. Which do you like best?

Some number of spades? 2? 3? 4? Other?

3◊ a mini-splinter showing a 3 or 5 level spade raise?

4◊? A 4-level splinter spade raise

4♣? A good 6-card source of tricks with four spades?

I like 4◊, since you might make slam opposite four spades to the jack and the club king. With stronger clubs, 4♣ would be a good bid.

Over 4◊, South bids 4NT, then 7♠ after North responds 5◊, 0 or 3 Keycards. The trump queen is hopefully not an issue with ten trump.

NO HCP, BUT BIDDING AWAY

```
                    ♠ Q 8 4 3
                    ♡ 9 6 3 2
                    ◇ 4
                    ♣ K 7 4 3
   ♠ J 10 6 5                        ♠ 9 2
   ♡ 10 5                            ♡ J
   ◇ A 10 9                          ◇ K J 8 6 5 2
   ♣ J 6 5 2                         ♣ Q 10 9 8
                    ♠ A K 7
                    ♡ A K Q 8 7 4
                    ◇ Q 7 3
                    ♣ A
```

South	North	
2♣	2◇*	* Waiting
2♡	4◇^	^ Splinter raise of hearts
4NT	5◇*	* 0 or 3 Keycards
6♡	All Pass	

North certainly doesn't have a plethora of HCP. But you never know when you have the 'right' hand. South's problem you can see is the diamond suit.

If North makes the lazy raise to 3♡, which should show trump support and an outside card, or even worse, raises to 4♡, will South bid again? Is there safety at the 5-level?

But with the 4◇ splinter, South's worries vanish. Now facing a singleton, she has a hand suitable to ask for Keycards, just in case that singleton is an ace.

North probably didn't think she was going to be making a slam try when she first picked up her hand. Who needs HCP? Easy game, this bridge.

PLEASE STOP

Jim
♠ K Q 3 2
♡ K Q J 10 3
◇ Q 5
♣ 6 4

♠ A 10 8 4   ♠ J 9 6 5
♡ 7 5 4 2   ♡ 6
◇ 9 4   ◇ 7 6 3 2
♣ A Q 5   ♣ K 10 9 3

Jim's New Student (No names)
♠ 7
♡ A 9 8
◇ A K J 10 8
♣ J 8 7 2

North	South	
1♡	2◇*	* Game forcing, so far so good
2♡*	3♠^	* Default bid, nothing else to bid
		^ My new toy Jim just taught me, a delayed Splinter raise.
		"Already I'm sorry," thinks Jim.
4♡*	5◇^	* Worst spade holding, please stop bidding
		^ Cue bid, I love my hand, I don't care what you think
5♡*		* The 5th and final heart, down one.

Of course South should have passed 4♡. this is consistent with most bidding decisions. When you have finished showing your hand, respect your partner's decision.

If you really had something extra, you might have bid again, or have bid in a different manner. On this hand South was finished after bidding 3♠.

AFTER MICHAEL'S CUE BID

                       ♠ A 10 6
                       ♡ 10 6 5
                       ◊ K 9
                       ♣ A Q 8 4 3

        ♠ K 8 3   ♠ Q J 9 7 5
        ♡ J 9 4 3   ♡ A K Q 8 2
        ◊ J 7 5 2   ◊ 10 3
        ♣ 9 5   ♣ 10

                       ♠ 4 2
                       ♡ 7
                       ◊ A Q 8 6 4
                       ♣ K J 7 6 2

North	East	South	West	
1♣	2♣^	3♡*	P	^ Majors * Splinter, Clubs with a short heart
4◊*	P	4NT^	P	* Keycard ask in clubs ^ Two, no queen
6♣	All Pass			

South had a good hand, and hoping North had more than three clubs made a big club raise, showing heart shortness on the way.

North was looking at three small hearts. This pair was playing that the suit above the minor was the Keycard asking bid, keeping the responses from going past 5♣.

When South showed two Keycards, North could bid 6♣. A good slam, only needing diamonds to be no worse than 4-2.

FIGHTING THEIR PREEMPT

♠ K J 8 5
♡ K Q 8 4
♢ 4
♣ A Q J 7

♠ 1 0 6 2   ♠ 9 7 4 3
♡ 7   ♡ 9 6 5 2
♢ A K Q 8 7 5   ♢ J 9 2
♣ 1 0 3 2   ♣ 9 4

♠ A Q
♡ A J 10 3
♢ 10 6 3
♣ K 8 6 5

South	West	North	East	
1♣	2♢*	Dbl^	P	* Weak ^ Majors
2♡	P	4♢*	P	* Splinter raise of hearts, short diamond
4♠*	P	5♡^	P	* Kickback Keycard ask in hearts
6♡	All Pass			^ Two Keycards and the trump queen

South's hand markedly improved when North showed a singleton diamond and extra values. Looking at three little diamonds, he asked for Keycards and bid the slam.

Notice the advantage of using Kickback, 4♠ as the asking bid in hearts rather than 4NT. Suppose you asked needing three and partner showed two with the queen. You would be at 5♠, when 5♡ might be the limit of the deal. With 4♠ as the ask, as in the minors, the response can never get too high.

If South had a different hand, something like:

♠ A Q 7   ♡ J 9 5 2   ♢ K Q 3   ♣ 10 6 3

he would know his diamond cards were idle and stop in 4♡.

SYSTEM PROBLEMS

As South, your hand is # 1, ♠ A K J 7 5 ♡ K 3 ◇ K Q J 10 5 ♣ 8

The auction proceeds:

South	North	
1♠	2♣*	* Game forcing
3◇		

Do you have the hand above, big hand with diamonds, or:

2, ♠ A K J 7 5   ♡ K 7 3   ◇ 6   ♣ K Q 10 9 a splinter raise of clubs

Actually, both of these treatments are in use. The latter is becoming more popular, the splinter raise.

Mike Lawrence said that in his Two Over One book, he played it as hand # 1, diamonds. But by the time he got around to putting his system on a CD Rom, he was playing it as hand # 2.

Something to discuss. I much prefer hand 2. In Two over One, jumping is to be avoided as much as possible. That's the whole idea of the system.

GETTING RIGHT IN THERE

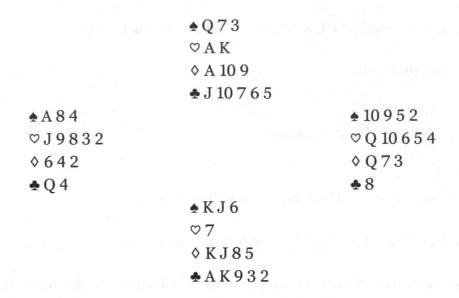

♠ Q 7 3
♡ A K
◇ A 10 9
♣ J 10 7 6 5

♠ A 8 4
♡ J 9 8 3 2
◇ 6 4 2
♣ Q 4

♠ 10 9 5 2
♡ Q 10 6 5 4
◇ Q 7 3
♣ 8

♠ K J 6
♡ 7
◇ K J 8 5
♣ A K 9 3 2

North opened 1♣ and South had to choose a bid. 3♡ is a perfect description. Clubs and a singleton heart, stronger than starting with a forcing inverted club raise, then showing shortness (see system notes under Meet The Minors).

North bids 3NT, suggesting a duplication of values in hearts opposite South's shortness. Too bad; with the right hand, South had visions of a slam in clubs.

Playing inverted minors, raising and then showing shortness is usually limited to hands of 12-14 HCP. With extra values, use an immediate splinter.

BROKE BUT TRUSTING

                          ♠ 9 8 6 5 4 2
                          ♡ 7 4 3
                          ◊ 3
                          ♣ K J 4

    ♠ Q 7   ♠ J
    ♡ A Q 10 8   ♡ K J 9 6 5
    ◊ J 8 6 5 2   ◊ Q 10 7 4
    ♣ Q 8   ♣ A 6 5

                          ♠ A K 10 3
                          ♡ 2
                          ◊ A K 9
                          ♣ 10 9 7 3 2

South opened 1♣ and North bid 1♠. South bid 3♡, a mini-splinter raise to 3♠,
showing four spades, 15- 17 support points and a singleton heart.
If you were North, would you bid or pass?

It depends how you think about bridge. A point counter would look at his hand
and say, "I have only 4 HCP" and stop there. A thinking bridge player would think
this way: "What have I got? What have I shown?" North could have a hand like this:
♠ Q 6 4 2   ♡ K 7 4   ◊ Q 6 4   ♣ 8 6 5 with 7 HCP and sign off in 3♠.

Instead, he has six, count'em, six spades, his own singleton, and three little in the
suit partner just splintered into. I would bid 4♠ in a flash, hoping I wasn't missing a
slam (just kidding).

As the late expert Bernie Chazen always used to say, "If all you do is count your
HCP, you will never become a bridge player."

FIND A BETTER WAY

♠ K J 7 5 2
♥ 7 4
♦ A J 7
♣ K 6 4

♠ 6 4 3   ♠ 8
♥ K J 8 6   ♥ Q 10 5 2
♦ Q 9 5 4   ♦ K 10 8 6 3 2
♣ 8 5   ♣ J 2

♠ A Q 10 9
♥ A 9 3
♦ void
♣ A Q 10 9 7 3

South	North	
1♣	1♠	
4♦*	4♠	* Splinter raise of spades
All Pass		

North knew South had a good hand, but with his diamond holding not working and two small hearts, was reluctant to move forward. And what could he bid?

Who was to blame for missing a grand slam, let alone a small slam?

Just because you have a new toy doesn't mean you have to trot it out. A better auction which perhaps better describes the South hand is:

South	North	
1♣	1♠	
4♣*	5♣^	* Long clubs, 4 spades, extras ^ Club fit
5♥	6♠	
7♠	All Pass	

Notice how without the discovery of the club fit, it's very hard to find the trick taking potential of the combined hands. You don't have to bid seven, but at least reach six spades.

NOTHING OPPOSITE NOTHING

$\spadesuit$ 2
$\heartsuit$ 9 7 6 3
$\diamond$ K Q 9 6 5 2
$\clubsuit$ A Q

$\spadesuit$ 10 9 8 7 4 3
$\heartsuit$ A K 8
$\diamond$ 8
$\clubsuit$ 9 6 5

$\spadesuit$ K 6 5
$\heartsuit$ Q J 10 5 2
$\diamond$ J
$\clubsuit$ K 8 4 2

$\spadesuit$ A Q J
$\heartsuit$ 4
$\diamond$ A 10 7 4 3
$\clubsuit$ J 10 7 3

North	East	South	West	
1$\diamond$	1$\heartsuit$	3$\heartsuit$*	4$\heartsuit$	* Splinter raise of diamonds
4NT	P	5$\heartsuit$	P	
6$\diamond$	All Pass			

After East's overcall, South could cue bid 2$\heartsuit$ to show a good hand with diamonds. But having splinters available, 3$\heartsuit$ is more descriptive.

A good slam, reached with eleven opposite twelve and could have been even less.

BLAST OR SCIENCE?

```
                        ♠ 10 9 6 4 3
                        ♡ 10 8 2
                        ◇ A Q 7 5
                        ♣ 3
♠ A K J 2                                        ♠ Q 8 7 5
♡ 5 4                                            ♡ Q
◇ J 9 2                                          ◇ 10 8 6
♣ J 9 8 7                                        ♣ K 10 6 5 4
                        ♠ void
                        ♡ A K J 9 7 6 3
                        ◇ K 4 3
                        ♣ A Q 2
```

South has a very good hand. He opened 1♡ and North raised to 2♡. Now what? One reasonable bid is 6♡.and hope the hands fit well. This is not as silly as it sounds. This has the advantage of leaving the opening leader with no information. A favorable opening lead may let you make a no-play slam.

What about a more scientific auction?

South	North	
1♡	2♡	
3♠*	4◇^	* Self splinter for hearts ^ Cue bid for hearts
4♠^	5NT*	^ Void * Interested in seven, club control
7♡	All Pass	

South splinters with 3♠, then rebids 4♠ showing a void. With nothing wasted in spades, North is going to slam. Bidding 5♣ would show the club ace; 5NT should show a club control. South bids the grand slam.

NO CONFUSION

♠ A Q 9 8
♡ K J 2
◊ Q 9 6 2
♣ Q 3

♠ 6 5
♡ Q 10 4 3
◊ K 8 7 4 3
♣ 8 6

♠ J 7 4
♡ 9 8 7 6
◊ A J 10
♣ 9 5 4

♠ K 10 3 2
♡ A 5
◊ 5
♣ A K J 10 7 2

North	South	
1◊	2♣*	* Game forcing
2♠	4◊^	^ Splinter raise of spades (Partner, not diamonds, please)
4NT	5◊*	* 0 or 3 (If I bid them once more, I may end up playing them)
5♠*	6♣^	* Pass if 0, bid if 3 ^ 3 plus the ♣ king
6♠	All Pass	

What's the best bid for South after North opens 1◊? Some players bid their major first. That is so wrong. Bid your long suit first; you will find your major fit later. Assuming you are playing 2/1, (please tell me yes), the auction will flow.

When North bids spades, not a reverse after South's 2/1 club bid, South's hand just got even better. Will North think 4◊ is diamonds?

Let's hope not. Remember if a bid, in this case 3◊, would be natural and forcing, then 4◊ cannot be diamonds. It must be a splinter raise of spades.

FIVE LEVEL MINI

$$\spadesuit\ 9\ 7\ 6\ 5\ 3$$
$$\heartsuit\ Q\ 8\ 7$$
$$\diamondsuit\ Q\ 9\ 4$$
$$\clubsuit\ K\ 8$$

♠ J	♠ Q 10 8
♡ 9 6 5 2	♡ 10 4 3
◊ 10 7 6 5 3 2	◊ A K J 8
♣ Q 7	♣ 10 4 2

$$\spadesuit\ A\ K\ 4\ 2$$
$$\heartsuit\ A\ K\ J$$
$$\diamondsuit\ \text{void}$$
$$\clubsuit\ A\ J\ 9\ 6\ 5\ 3$$

South opened 1♣ and North bid 1♠. South, having just learned splinters, bid 4◊. North was not interested and bid 4♠. South is still trying to decide what to do next if anything.

How would you have handled the South hand?

A perfect hand for a mini-splinter 3 or 5 bid. Look at this auction:

South	North
1♣	1♠
3 ◊*	3♠ * A mini-splinter, usually a raise to 3♠, sometimes a 5♠ bid
4 ◊^	5♣* ^ Void, 3◊ was a 5♠ bid * Asks about hearts, the unbid suit
6♡*	6♠ * First round control
All Pass	

Opposite a 5-level drive and a diamond void, North appreciates his fifth trump and club king. Five spades asks South to bid a slam if he has a control in the unbid suit, hearts. South has first round control, but North is interested in six, not seven.

THIS TIME I'M GOING

$$\spadesuit \text{ J 10 4}$$
$$\heartsuit \text{ 10 8 7 6 5 4}$$
$$\diamond \text{ A K 8 5}$$
$$\clubsuit \text{ void}$$

<table>
<tr><td>♠ 7 5 2</td><td></td><td>♠ K 6 3</td></tr>
<tr><td>♡ Q</td><td></td><td>♡ J 2</td></tr>
<tr><td>◊ Q 9 7 6 4</td><td></td><td>◊ J 10 3 2</td></tr>
<tr><td>♣ J 8 6 4</td><td></td><td>♣ Q 10 3 2</td></tr>
</table>

$$\spadesuit \text{ A Q 9 8}$$
$$\heartsuit \text{ A K 9 3}$$
$$\diamond \text{ void}$$
$$\clubsuit \text{ A K 9 7 5}$$

South opened 1♣ and North bid 1♡. South's 3♦ bid was a 3 or 5 mini-splinter. North accepted South 'game try', bidding 4♡.

"Well," thought South. "If you want to be in game over my 3-level bid, let's see what you think of my 5-level bid."

The auction continued:

South	North	
1♣	1♡	
3◊*	4♡^	* A 3 or 5 level mini-splinter
		^ Accepting game opposite a 3-level splinter
4♠*	5◊*	* Cue bids
6♣*	6◊*	
7♡	All Pass	

51

Major Suit Game Tries

To ask or tell, that is the question. After a major has been opened and raised to the two level, opener has three choices. He can pass, bid game, or solicit help from partner. Often it's a marginal decision and opener wants to make a game try. It's almost always a question of where partner's HCP are, not how many. He already knows how many. It's not going to change. Imagine the following:

<table>
<tr><td>Dummy # 1</td><td>Dummy # 2</td></tr>
<tr><td>♦ K 3 2   ♣ 4 3 2</td><td>♦ 4 3 2   ♣ K 3 2</td></tr>
<tr><td>Declarer</td><td>Declarer</td></tr>
<tr><td>♦ 6 5 4   ♣ A Q 10</td><td>♦ 7 6 5   ♣ A Q 10</td></tr>
</table>

With dummy # 1, on a bad day, declarer could have three diamond losers and two club losers. With dummy # 2, declarer has three losers.

There are many types of game tries. The most common include long suit game tries (LSGT), help suit game tries (HSGT) which should be called weak suit game tries, short suit game tries (SSGT), attributed to Kaplan-Sheinwold, combined long and short suit (CLSHST), 2NT game try (2NTGT), Kokish Game Try Bids, Nagy's Game Try, Reverse Romex, North Carolina Game Tries (NCGT), and others.

For purposes of this book, we will focus only on Short Suit Game Tries. The above list increases in complexity as it goes on. However, one has to admire the North Carolina variety, popularized by the expert Jerry Helms. It's simple; bid game and hope you make it.

SSGT – With this agreement, a new suit by opener shows shortness and asks responder to evaluate his hand in the light of opener's shortness. Responder can return to the major at the three level, a sign-off, or bid a new suit room permitting as a counter game try, showing values in the suit bid.

Opener has another option that instead of 'telling', he can 'ask'. Let's say opener does this by bidding the next step, ie; 2♠ after 1♥ - 2♥, and 2NT after 1♠ - 2♠. Both ask responder "do you have any shortness?"

And you will recall our method of replying, which may likely differ from other reading material you have seen. Let's use 1st step 'no', etc, up-the-line. (Standard replies differ- three of the trump suit says no, naming the suit etc,) but I think up-the-line takes away all memory-your choice.

Note that over spades, it's easy; 2NT starts the ask. But over hearts, since 2♠ starts the ask, 1♡-2♡-2NT is a tell, club shortness. Remember, it's up-the-line. Just to show you how confusing standard is, 2NT here would be spade shortness., then club shortness. Are you kidding me?

For example: ♠ A K J 5 4   ♡ K 8 6   ◇ K J 7 5   ♣ 7, after a 1♠ - 2♠ auction, bid 3♣ showing shortness. While this is a telling bid, it does not give the opponents too much information since if the suit is led it is not too damaging and you have strength in the unbid suits. A possible disadvantage is an opponent may double with length and strength in the short suit and the opponents may find a good sacrifice.

We would prefer this method to either the LSGT or HSGT. However, holding:
♠ A K J 5 4   ♡ 8 6   ◇ 9 7   ♣ A Q J 7

or

♠ A K J 9 7   ♡ A K   ◇ 9 7   ♣ 8 7 6 2
there is no shortness. Now you do not tell but instead you would ask partner to show shortness.

2NT as a game try is a less common alternative method suggested by Marty Bergen in his excellent book "Better Bidding with Bergen, Volume I." Marty suggested using 2NT as an asking bid for both hearts and spades, asking responder to show shortness.

Some suggested guidelines for responding to partner's SSGT are as follows:

1. If holding three losers in the short suit, bid game.
2. If holding ace and two other losers in the short suit, bid game.
3. Absent either of the above, sign-off at the 3-level of the agreed major.

For example, after 1♠ - 2♠ and opener makes a SSGT in clubs:

Opener: ♠ A K 10 9 3   ♡ K J 2   ◇ A J 9 2   ♣ 2

a) ♠ QJ6 ♡ Q 9 4 3 ◇ K 4   ♣ J 10 9 4 bid 4♠, your red suit honors are good
a) ♠ QJ4 ♡ 10 9 4 3 ◇ 8 7 6   ♣ K J 6 bid 3♠, your clubs are not working
b) ♠ J742 ♡ Q 7   ◇ Q 10 8 ♣ A 10 9 3 bid 4♠, your club ace is working.

Summary: Notice it's always the next bid starts the 'ask', all others are 'tells'.

1♠ - 2♠	1♡ - 2♡
3♣ - shortness	2NT - club shortness
3 ◇ - shortness	3♣ - diamond shortness
3 ♡ - shortness	3◇ - heart shortness
2NT - asks for shortness	2♠ - asks for shortness
3♣ - none	2NT - none
3 ◇ - club shortness	3♣ - club shortness
3 ♡ - diamond shortness	3◇ - diamond shortness
3♠ - heart shortness	3♡ - heart shortness

There are many types of game tries. I think SSGT are easy to use, require little effort (even the caddy can spot a singleton), and just discuss with your partner(s) what it takes to accept. There will always be times where you will wish you were playing some other system. This is true in all aspects of bidding.

Hand evaluation is a fluid, constantly changing affair. A good raise can lose value when your honor cards are not working. Also, the opponents may interfere, a topic not discussed here. It's mostly important to have a method you both are comfortable with. Try to avoid anything that requires memory.

One big fault with playing SSGT alone is sometimes you need to make a long-suit game try. There are ways of doing both, beyond the scope of this book.

I recommend a recent article in the Bridge World "The Long and Short of It."

ON THE SAME PAGE

$$\spadesuit\,K\,Q\,9\,2$$
$$\heartsuit\,Q\,8\,2$$
$$\diamond\,8\,5\,3\,2$$
$$\clubsuit\,J\,3$$

♠ 10 8 7   ♠ A 4 3
♡ 9 6   ♡ 10 7 5
◊ J 10 7 4   ◊ A K Q 9
♣ Q 9 7 4   ♣ 10 8 5

♠ J 6 5
♡ A K J 4 3
◊ 6
♣ A K 6 2

After North raised South's opening 1♡ to 2♡, South thought about blasting into 4♡, but instead made a SSGT by showing his singleton diamond. He bid 3♣, hoping his new partner was on the same page.

He could see her thinking (always a good sign), counting up-the-line and knew that he was showing a singleton diamond. He could almost see her lips going "2NT is clubs, 3♣ is diamonds, etc.".

She bid 4♡. "I read the same book, partner," said North.

IT'S AN ACE, BUT

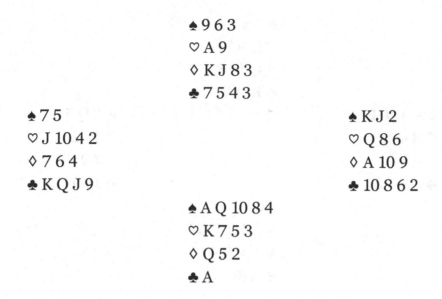

♠ 9 6 3
♡ A 9
◇ K J 8 3
♣ 7 5 4 3

♠ 7 5
♡ J 10 4 2
◇ 7 6 4
♣ K Q J 9

♠ K J 2
♡ Q 8 6
◇ A 10 9
♣ 10 8 6 2

♠ A Q 10 8 4
♡ K 7 5 3
◇ Q 5 2
♣ A

South opened 1♠ and North raised to 2♠. Would you try for game? Close, singleton aces aren't the greatest, but that's what the dealing machine gave you.

South bid 3♣, a singleton. What do you think about doing that with an ace? We talked about this when we talked about splinters. Should you splinter with a stiff ace? Some experts like Jerry Helms say sure, others are horrified. I think it's the best description of your hand.

On this hand you strike gold. What a surprise! Four small. Not a 30 point deck since you have the ace of that suit, but from North's point of view, he couldn't bid 4♠ fast enough even with his meager trump holding.

A CLASSIC THIRTY FOUR POINTER

        ♠ 9 8 7 6
        ♡ Q 9 3
        ◊ Q 10 8
        ♣ K Q 3

♠ K J 10 2   ♠ A Q 5 4
♡ 8 4   ♡ 10 2
◊ 6 3 2   ◊ J 9 5
♣ J 5 4 2   ♣ 10 9 7 5

        ♠ 3
        ♡ A K J 7 6 5
        ◊ A K 7 4
        ♣ A 8

South opened 1♡ and North raised to 2♡. South, always bidding at least game, first bid 3◊ showing spade shortness (2♠ would have been an 'asking' bid). North with nothing wasted in spades, bid 4♡. South checked for Keycards and bid 6♡.

Another option for South was to self-splinter. A 3♠ bid would have been at least a 4♡ bid with spade shortness. However, a subsequent 4NT might have suggested a spade void.

A good slam with 19 opposite 9 HCP. North certainly had the perfect hand, four small opposite South's singleton. The classic 34 point deck. West led, South claimed if no one was ruffing.

DESTRUCTIVE RAISES?

```
              ♠ A 8 7 4 3
              ♡ 10 5 4 3
              ◇ 9
              ♣ Q 4 3
  ♠ K 10                        ♠ Q J 9 2
  ♡ K 8                         ♡ J 9
  ◇ J 8 7 6 3                   ◇ A 10 5 2
  ♣ 9 8 5 2                     ♣ K 10 7
              ♠ 6 5
              ♡ A Q 7 6 2
              ◇ K Q 4
              ♣ A J 6
```

South opened 1♡, reluctant to open 1NT with two small spades. North raised to 2♡. With hopes for game, South bid 2♠, asking if North had any shortness, and if so, to bid it up-the-line.

North bid 3◇, the third step. 2NT would have said "No", then suits in order up-the-line. That was not what South wanted to hear. He signed off in 3♡, plenty high, and hoped he could make that.

"Partner, I thought we were playing constructive raises," said South.

WRONG ONE

```
                    ♠ 10
                    ♡ Q 10 7 5
                    ◇ K 9 3
                    ♣ K J 6 5 3
♠ A 8 6 5 2                          ♠ Q 9 7 4
♡ 6                                  ♡ 9 8 4
◇ Q 8 6 5 4                          ◇ A J 10
♣ 9 2                                ♣ Q 10 4
                    ♠ K J 3
                    ♡ A K J 3 2
                    ◇ 7 2
                    ♣ A 8 7
```

South opened 1♡ rather than 1NT, concerned about his diamond holding. When North bid 2♡ however, he was interested in game. He bid 2♠, asking if North had any shortness, perhaps hoping for club shortness?

North bid 3♡ showing spade shortness. Not what the doctor ordered.

South was sorry he had asked and wanted to go back to 2♡. Holding ♠KJx opposite a singleton is probable the worst possible holding. However, with enough high card strength, he scampered home with nine tricks.

SUGARPLUMS

```
                    ♠ J 9 8 6
                    ♡ Q 7 5 4 2
                    ◊ A Q 4
                    ♣ 4
    ♠ 10 2                              ♠ 5 4
    ♡ 8 6                               ♡ K J 9 3
    ◊ J 9 7 5                           ◊ K 10 8
    ♣ K J 9 6 5                         ♣ A 8 7 3
                    ♠ A K Q 7 3
                    ♡ A 10
                    ◊ 6 3 2
                    ♣ Q 10 2
```

South opened 1♠ and North bid 2♠. South bid 2NT, asking North if she had any shortness. On a good day, he would find North with a singleton diamond.

This wasn't one of those days. North bid 3◊ showing a singleton club (3♣ would have said no shortness). Of course, South was so excited to see the 3◊ card he forgot what he was playing.

Thinking partner had a singleton diamond, visions of sugarplums danced in his head. Could there be a slam in this 30-34 point deal? He would need North to have the perfect hand; ♣AK and ♡K. But if he had that hand plus a singleton, he would likely have made a limit raise.

And what had Freddy told him? Never play partner for the perfect hand. He signed off in 4♠ and said, "I don't think we missed a slam, partner."

After he went down one, North said, "You were at least right about your prediction, partner. Better study your notes."

Other Major Shortness

JACOBY 2NT – A FORCING MAJOR SUIT RAISE

One of the most common conventions in use is the Jacoby 2NT Forcing Raise after partner has opened one of a major. This shows game forcing values and at least four trumps with 2NT as the trigger over one of a major opening.

As happens with most conventions, this convention sprouts different versions. The use of ambiguous, singleton-or-void, three-level rebids was not in the original version. Amalya Kearse, in her book Bridge Conventions Complete, defined three of a new suit as a singleton and a jump to four of a new suit as a void.

In the now more popular version, opener's rebid of a new suit at the 3-level is shortness, a singleton or void. This says nothing about the strength of opener's hand; further exploration will reveal the partnership's assets. Should opener rebid this suit again at the 4-level, that would indicate a void.

The only exception to showing your shortness is a second suit which is a source of tricks. For example, holding ♠ A Q J 4 3   ♡ Q 4   ◊ A K J 10 9   ♣ 2, after 1♠ - 2NT, opener should bid 4◊. Opener has shortness somewhere, but the source of tricks, the feature of the hand takes priority.

With ♠ A Q J 4 3   ♡ K J   ◊ A J 9 4 2   ♣ 2, after 1♠ - 2NT, one should bid 3♣ showing shortness. The same shape, the same HCP strength, but the feature of the hand is shortness, not a source of tricks.

Some pairs play different responses. For example, rather than force opener to reveal his hand, many experienced partnerships use the following:

1 Major – 2NT (Same, a forcing major suit raise)

    3♣ - all minimums   Responder may now choose to sign off in game. Or

        3◊ - Do you have any shortness?

            3♡ - No

            3♠, 3NT, 4♣ - singletons up-the-line, club, diamond, other major

      3◊ - extras, with shortness

        3♡ - where?

            3♠, 3NT, 4♣ - singletons up-the-line, club, diamond, other major

This has the advantage of declarer not revealing his hand unless responder asks, meaning he has extras and serious slam interest.

Other options: Some pairs prefer to keep 2NT as a natural bid. There is a lot of merit to this. These pairs have different forcing major raises, sometimes referred to as FeMuR. Having 2NT as a natural game forcing bid is very useful when partner opens a major and you have a game forcing balanced hand with a doubleton in his suit.

It avoids the need to manufacture a 2/1 response.
For example, after partner opens 1♠ and you hold:

♠ Q 4   ♡ A Q 6 4   ◊ A 8 6 4   ♣ Q 6 4

since 2♡ shows a 5-card suit, and 2◊ suggests the same, some would bid 2♣ to create a game force, an ideal hand for 2NT, natural and game forcing. But I digress.

Getting back to other forcing raises, for example, some pairs play that 1♡ - 2♠ and 1♠ - 3♣ are 'FeMur's'.

You can still show singletons using the methods described above, ie:
1♡ - 2♠ (a forcing heart raise)

3♣ - all minimums	3◊ can ask for shortness
3◊ - extras with shortness	3♡ can ask where
3♡ - extra, no shortness	

There are more responses in these systems, showing various other hands but we are focusing on shortness, so I have omitted them. They are readily available if requested. These systems have several advantages over the standard 2NT response.

A significant advantage of these systems is the ease of separating singletons from voids. If singletons are silver, voids are gold.

BERGEN MAJOR RAISES

Marty Bergen deserves great credit for inventing Bergen Major Suit Raises, which follow along with the Law of Total Tricks. In short, if you have nine trump in your combined hands, you have safety at the 3-level. Getting there and shutting out the opponents is at the heart of the matter.

A quick summary of Bergen raises is as follows:

1 Major – 3♣ shows single raise values with 4+ trump

1 Major – 3♦ shows limit raise values with 4+ trump

1 Major – 3 Major is preemptive, 4+ trump, too weak for 3♣

Some pairs reverse the first two responses. I usually ask them why? Do you think Marty tossed a coin as to which way he wanted the responses to be? There is a logical reason for doing it Marty's way.

Playing standard, when your partner makes a limit raise, such as 1♠-3♠, do you have a lot to think about? Usually not. But when the bidding goes 1♠ - 2♠, as we have seen, you often need room to make some type of game try.

Especially in hearts, how much room is there after 1♡ - 3♦? None. It's decision time, go or no go. Playing the way Marty invented provides the most room to explore.

But how can you explore? For example, after 1♡ - 3♣, a single raise, what is your only game try? 3♦, but what does that mean other than I'm interested in a game. It's not a Short Suit, a Long Suit, not anything other than "I'm interested."

So maybe we can do something about that. I would suggest the following, to make these game tries mean something.

AFTER ANY BERGEN RAISE, THE NEXT NON SIGN-OFF BID ASKS FOR SHORTNESS.

1♡/1♠ - 3♣

    3◇ - I'm interested in game; do you have any shortness
        3♡ - No (1st step). 3S, 3NT, 4C up-the-line singletons, C, D, other major.

Partner might just be trying for game. He might be slamming and really looking for a singleton. That's his business. Of course, if you have no singleton but love your hand, bid game yourself.

This can apply to any Bergen bid. Partner might be slamming. For example:

1♡-3◇

    3♠ the cheapest non-sign-off bid, asking for shortness.
        3NT – No, 4C, 4D, 4H C, D, other major singletons

1/♡/1♠ - 3♡/♠ (Preemptive)

    3NT- asks for shortness
        4♣ - no
        4◇, ♡, ♠ up-the-line, C, D, H other major

MIXED RAISES AND SINGLETONS

First, what is a mixed raise? If you are already comfortable with the concept of Bergen raises, you should incorporate mixed raises into your bidding system. It's very simple (yes, I know, I say that about everything) but here is the only thing you need to know.

When the opponents open one of anything and partner overcalls one of a major, a jump to three of a minor is a mixed raise by advancer. It shows single raise values and 4+ trump. But a mixed raise is always a jump. Therefore, it applies only when your right hand opponent either passes, bids 1NT, or doubles. It's basically a jump cue bid.

You hold Hand (a): ♠ J 10 9 5   ♡ K 3   ◊ K Q 7 2   ♣ 10 9 3

The auction has proceeded 1♣ - 1♠ (partner) – Dbl - ?

You have the values for a single raise but it's unlikely you will be allowed to play in 2♠. Your side has at least nine trumps so you want to get to the three level as quickly as possible. Bidding 3♠ would be preemptive, a hand like:
Hand (b)   ♠ K J 9 5   ♡ 5 3   ◊ J 10 7 4 3   ♣ 9 3

Cue bidding would overstate your values. In a competitive auction, you want to help partner do the right thing so it's important to accurately portray your hand.
A jump cue, the mixed raise tells the story.

*** But wait! Let's add a twist. Forget which minor was opened. Play that both jumps to 3♣ and 3◊ are mixed raises. 3♣ has a singleton somewhere, 3◊ does not. Over 3♣, partner can ask with 3◊ in the usual fashion. You can remember which is which. There is more room over 3♣.

Suppose partner holds: ♠ A Q 7 6 4 3   ♡ A 6 4   ◊ 6 5   ♣ K 4

If you bid 3♠, and the opponents bid 4♡, he will be wondering who can make what. If he could be sure you had the weaker hand above, Hand (b), a 4♠ sacrifice could be right. If you hold the first hand, Hand (a), with some values, he will prefer to defend, hoping to beat 4♡.

Mixed raises also apply in the following situations, in exactly the same mode.

1. After partner opens one of a major and your RHO doubles, 3♣ and 3◊ are both mixed raises, with and without shortness.
2. After exactly 1♡ - 1♠ - 3♣ and 3◊ are mixed raises.

As Karen Walker pointed out in her excellent discussion of mixed raises in the ACBL Bulletin, October, 2012, many experts advise you can't have too many ways to raise partner's major suit bids. Being specific in your meaning will help insure the opponents will be doing the guessing, not your partner.

The extra twist about the 2-way mixed raise with and without shortness is a big extra and worth incorporating at no cost.

Let's look at two example deals.

MIXED RAISE

Both vul   ♠ A 10 8 7 5
North dealer   ♡ A K 3
        ◇ Q 8 4
        ♣ 8 7

♠ J 6   ♠ K 3
♡ 6 5   ♡ Q 9 8 4
◇ J 10 7   ◇ A 6 5 3
♣ A 10 9 5 4 3   ♣ K J 6

        ♠ Q 9 4 2
        ♡ J 10 7 2
        ◇ K 9 2
        ♣ Q 2

North	East	South	West
1♠	Dbl	2♠	3♣
P	P	?	

Should South take the push now and bid the third spade based on his fourth spade? If so, would E/W double? Down one, -200 would be a very poor result.

E/W would probably double to protect their equity. If they can make 3♣ for +110, then +100 is not enough.

But suppose the auction proceeds as such:

North	East	South	West	
1♠	Dbl	3◇*	?	* A mixed raise, constructive in spades, no shortness

Now what? West is not bidding 4♣. North will bid 3♠. E/W are shut out of bidding. Who will double? With most sensible lines, N/S can make 2♠, E/W can make 3♣.

SILENCING THE OPPONENTS

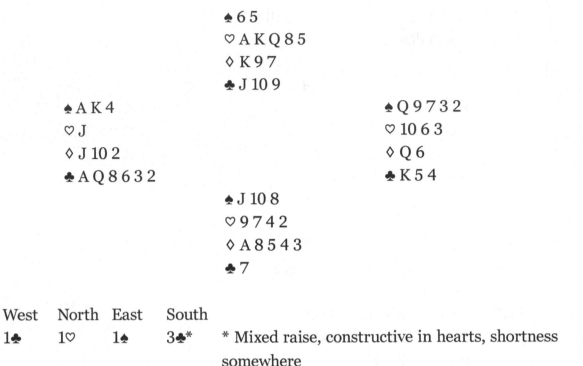

♠ 6 5			
♡ A K Q 8 5			
◊ K 9 7			
♣ J 10 9			

♠ A K 4   ♠ Q 9 7 3 2
♡ J   ♡ 10 6 3
◊ J 10 2   ◊ Q 6
♣ A Q 8 6 3 2   ♣ K 5 4

                          ♠ J 10 8
                          ♡ 9 7 4 2
                          ◊ A 8 5 4 3
                          ♣ 7

West	North	East	South
1♣	1♡	1♠	3♣*	* Mixed raise, constructive in hearts, shortness somewhere
P	3♡	All Pass		

South has to decide what to bid. He has single raise values, but four trumps and a singleton. He does not want to get into a heart versus spade fight. Preempting with an ace by bidding 3♡ feels wrong.

This is a perfect hand for a mixed raise. A jump to 3♣ or 3◊ describes this hand, the former shows shortness, the latter denying.

If North had a better hand, he might bid 3◊ asking where South's singleton is. After all, ♣J109 opposite a singleton ♣7 is usually very good. North knowing South lacks limit raise values signs off in 3♡.

Notice it's difficult for East-West to get into this auction. After all, 4♠ is a pretty good contract.

DRURY AND SINGLETONS

To conclude our discussion of the majors and singletons, let's see a few examples in Drury auctions.

The definition of Drury is a passed hand that is too good for a single raise. That might be a balanced hand with 10 – 11 HCP such as:

♠ Q 7 5   ♡ A 7 5   ◇ K Q 6 4   ♣ 9 6 4

As a passed hand, and partner opens 1♡ or 1♠. I would bid 2♣, Drury, asking partner to describe his hand.

Or a hand such as ♠ A 6 5 3   ♡ A 8 6 4   ◇ 8   ♣ 10 7 5 2

I would Drury after either 1♡ or 1♠. It's a minimum, but if you raised to two, and partner goes into the tank and finally passes, you know you missed game.

When might a passed hand have something special with shortness?

The auction Pass – 1 Major
2NT is the biggest passed hand raise. After all, now you are committing to the three level regardless. This bid should show a real maximum passed hand, 4+ trump, AND a singleton somewhere.

As a matter of note, also by a passed hand,
1 major – 3♣ (and 3◇ if playing 2-way Drury) are natural, 9-11 HCP, and almost always have a singleton in partner's major.
Otherwise, you would probable bid 1NT.

Opener can splinter after Drury;

North	South		
P	1♠		
2♣*	3◇^	* Drury, limit raise in spades	^ Diamond shortness, extras

"Spiral" and The Lost Singleton

An often overlooked source of shortness by most players occurs when using the so-called 'Spiral' convention, first described by this author in the "ACBL Bulletin" November, 2009, page 30, under the Bidding Lab.

Many players use a simplified version of 3344. The auction of one of a minor- one of a major-two of the major is generic. It doesn't matter what the suits are. 2NT by responder asks for more description about opener's hand. Nothing is given away about declarer's hand since opener will likely be the dummy. But besides just the 3344 responses, consider the further depth of the convention as described below.

After the generic auction: 1 either minor – 1 either Major

2 that Major – 2NT Artificial inquiry

3♣ - minimum with three trump. Non-forcing, a possible place to play.

   3◊ - To play, if opener opened 1◊. When responder had four of his major and four plus length in opener's minor, three of the minor is usually better than the 4-3 major fit.

3◊ - maximum with three trump, game forcing. But overlooked is that this bid promises a singleton or void somewhere.

   3♡ - where is your shortage? (step responses, but no 'no' response).

   3♠ - other minor 3NT – Other major

3♡ - minimum with four trump and no shortage, non-forcing.

   Pass – To play 3♡   3♠ - To play in three spades

3♠ - maximum with four trump, game forcing, may or may not have shortage.

   3NT – Any shortage (Step responses)

   4 ♣ - No 4◊ other minor   4♡ - other major

3NT – maximum with three trump, but denies shortage. Compare to 3◊.

4 other minor* – minimum with four trump, singleton in suit bid.

4 of opener's minor* – minimum with four trump, singleton in other major.

   • Probably had a two and a half bid raise the first time

4 of major – maximum, 4 2 5 2, with 4 of the major, 5 of the minor

*** The search for shortness, I have found to be overlooked
by 99% of players in these auctions.

Meet The  Minors

Hello. Remember us? Yes, way back when you first started bridge you learned there were majors and minors. But since we were only 20 per trick while the big guys were 30 per trick, plus you needed to take eleven tricks for us to make game, we got left behind. The majors got all the attention- 5-card majors, 4-card majors, Bergen raises, Drury, Jacoby raises, etc, big deal. Or everybody is in 3NT no matter what their hand is.

Well, what about when it's wrong? Yes, I know you just forget about it, chalk it up to bad luck and go on to the next board saying it's just too complicated to get involved in all that other stuff. You just keep bidding 3NT with your eyes closed. Full speed ahead, damn the torpedoes.

Well, it's time to put a stop to this way of thinking. Good bidding systems do not have to be complicated. They just have to be logical and have a purpose. They need be consistent and in an orderly fashion that can be understood with little need for memorization.

Experts have long recognized the power of distribution, especially shortness. Most good bidding systems are constructed in a manner to be able to demonstrate shortness, so critical to accurate game and slam bidding. At the same time, being able to avoid NT when it's wrong is the other objective of good bidding tools. If you know that your partner knows you have shortness, yet still wants to be in NT, you can be comfortable passing. This is the essence of good minor suit bidding.

First let's examine some of the so-called rules we have been playing for years without a good reason for doing so. Maybe we can improve on some of these. The two most common 'misrules' are 1) with 4-4 in the minors, open one diamond, and 2) play that one of a minor – 2NT is invitational, using 3NT as forcing.

Why are so many of you playing this way? Let's see if we can figure out why, and see if there is a better way.

Before discussing shortness, it's necessary to go over a few points. Why on the ACBL convention card does it ask how many HCP for 1C-1NT? Why not 1 minor-1NT?

It's important to understand why there is a different range for a 1NT response to 1C compared to 1D.

Over 1C, 1 NT is usually played as 8-10 HCP, a constructive bid. Why?

Because with a weaker hand and four clubs you could raise, playing standard, or bid 1D. But over 1D, 1 NT is 6-10 HCP. Why?

1 C-? Kxx Jxx Qxxx Kxx This 9 HCP hand is a fine 1NT response. You could bid 1D but why bother? The hand screams notrump.

1C -? xxx Kxx Jxx Qxxx This 6 HCP hand however should worry about notrump, especially about being the declarer or being raised. But there is no problem. You can bid 1D, yes, your 3-card suit, and then pass partner's next bid or bid 2C.

But notice that over 1D, there may be nowhere to go. You have to bid 1NT with as little as 6 HCP. With xxx Kxx xxx QJxx your choice is 1NT. But with this hand over 1C, you can bid 1D and then pass the next bid or bid 2 C.

What does of this mean? What's the big deal? Well, the question has long been argued when you are 4-4 in the minors, which should you open? We know that when we are 3-3 we open 1C, and most of you when 4-4 open 1D.

But why? You are still often rebidding 1NT whenever you are 2=3=4=4 or 3=2=4=4. Of course, if your 3-card fragment looks strong and partner bids that suit you might raise with two small in the other major. But look how much easier it is for partner to bid over 1C. You won't lose the diamond suit; you can raise if you feel like it. And even with Axx Kxx xxxx AKx, do you really want to open 1D and receive a diamond lead if your LHO becomes the declarer? So open 1C.

Now let's discuss playing 1 minor - 2NT as forcing and you will see the advantages of opening 1C whenever possible. Life will get easier and your results will get better. How can this be bad?

WHY PLAY 1 MINOR - 2NT FORCING?

The main reason is to avoid 3NT when it is wrong. For example, playing 2NT invitational:

You open 1C with ♠ x ♡ KJ10x ◇ Q10x ♣ AQxxx and partner bids 3NT. Now what?

Or you open 1 minor with ♠ AQxx ♡ x ◇ AQxx ♣ Qxxx and partner bids 3NT. Now what?

Are you passing? Of course you are.

So now on the 1ˢᵗ hand you are in 3NT with:

♠ x	♡ KJ10x	◇ Q10x	♣ AQxxx opposite:
♠ J10x	♡ Qxx	◇ AKx	♣ Kxxx

And the 2ⁿᵈ hand you are in 3NT with:

♠ AQxx	♡ x	◇ AQxx	♣ Qxxx opposite:
♠ J10x	♡ Qxx	◇ Kxx	♣ AKxx

Here are two of the most normal hands and you are going down in 3NT, with plays for 5 (or 6C)! What went wrong?

What went wrong was using up too much bidding space. Opener was shut out of further describing his hand. We need to have a way to avoid 3NT when it is clearly wrong, yes?

By playing 2NT as forcing we can avoid this. The KEY is opener being able to show shortness which he can't over 3NT. And I will show you how in a moment.

Because you are already asking "What about invitational hands?"

A good question and of course I have a good answer.

When do we need 1 minor- 2NT as invitational? Well, for starters,

over 1C- NEVER! We can first bid 1D, then 2NT invitational.

For example: With Axx Qxx xxx AJxx (or 4 D's & 3 C's), an invitational hand, start with 1D, then bid 2NT.

The auction should go 1C- 1D- 1 Major- now 2NT, or 1C-1D-1NT-2NT.

What about over 1D? With 6-10 HCP we bid 1NT, and with 12+ HCP we bid 2NT forcing. So it's only with exactly 11 HCP over 1D that we have a problem.

Should we give up a whole system I'm going to show you to cater to this 1/100 hand?

No, we can play that 1D-1NT can be 6-11 instead of 6-10.

This is one of the reasons we should try to open 1C rather than 1D whenever possible. It's much easier to respond to 1C.

1C-1D-2D is natural & does NOT indicate a reverse by opener.

If you hate your hand, xx KQx xxx Jxxxx, over 1D, bid a

confident 1H, then pass partners next bid. Don't even think about 1NT.

Maybe by now you are asking "Where does this guy come up with this stuff? Who plays bridge like this?"

Well, ask any good (not your friend) pair how they play 1 minor – 2NT.

Let me show you a deal and see what you think.

This deal is from the ACBL Bulletin, November, 2013, that Mike Lawrence showed. That's a long time ago and Mike, one of the most respected teachers and coaches, is certainly someone to listen to.

```
                        ♠ A Q 8 4
                        ♡ 2
                        ◊ Q J 8
                        ♣ Q J 10 9 7
        ♠ 9 6 5                          ♠ K J 2
        ♡ Q J 10 8 5 4                   ♡ A K 7
        ◊ 10 4                           ◊ 9 7 6 5 2
        ♣ 8 6                            ♣ 5 3
                        ♠ 10 7 3
                        ♡ 9 6 3
                        ◊ A K 3
                        ♣ A K 4 2
```

North	South
1♣	3NT

North-South were playing 1 minor – 2NT as invitational so South bid 3NT. North had no reason to bid on, so he passed. The defense took the first six heart tricks.

Mike pointed out this is a common occurrence. Sometimes it works fine, other times not so fine. How should the auction have gone? Let's see.

North	South	
1♣	2NT*	* Game forcing, likely no 4-card major
3♡^	4♣	^ Shortness in hearts!
5♣	All Pass	

This article was from nine years ago. This is not new. Let's see how a minor – 2NT works.

The History of 1 Minor – 2NT:

Just as a matter of interest, here are some of the ways 1 minor – 2NT has been played:

ACOL – Invitational, 11 – 12 HCP, no four=card major

Goren – Game Force, 13 – 15 HCP, no four-card major

Kantar – Game Force, 13 – 15 HCP, often one or two four-card majors

Miles – Game Force, 13-15 or 18-19 HCP, no four-card major

Baron – Game Force, 16 -18 HCP, often one or two four-card majors

1 MINOR – 2NT UNDERSTANDINGS

After 1 minor – 2NT, game forcing, the major objective is deciding "is 3NT the right contract?" This is best done by showing shortness, not by telling partner and the opponents where your strength lies. Responder has a 'balanced' hand.

Your LHO, on lead, does not have a long, strong major; there was no overcall. Shortness is more important than fragments. Don't tell them what to lead.

THE MOST BASIC AGREEMENTS YOU WILL NEED

> 1♣ - 2NT 12-15 HCP or 18-19 (will raise 3NT to 4NT)
> 3♣ - Balanced club slam try, 6+ clubs
> 3◊, 3♡, 3♠ - Singletons
> 3NT – To play
> 4♡, 4♠ - Minimum, 5-6 with 6 clubs
> 4NT – Quantitative – 18+

1◊ - 2NT As above
> 3◊ - Balanced diamond slam try, 6+ diamonds
> 3♣, 3♡, 3♠ - Singletons
> 3NT – To play
> 4♡, 4♠ - Minimum, 5-6 with 6 diamonds
> 4NT – Quantitative, 18+

NOTE: 2NT is 12-15 or 18-19. But 1 minor – 3NT can be bid with 15+-17.

With a bit extra, you can probably cover partner's shortness if any. These basic agreements will cover almost all deals. More detailed agreements are available.

BASIC AGREEMENTS AFTER MINOR SUIT RAISES

After a minor suit has been raised, whether standard but especially playing inverted, and 3NT is in the picture, the same 'shortness' problem raises its' head.

It's important to play this sequence is forcing to three of the minor. Why? So opener need not have to jump to 3NT to show extras; his 2NT rebid must be forcing to allow responder another call.

Like we saw with 1 minor – 2NT, shortness is more important than bidding fragments. LHO didn't overcall so opener strives to rebid 2NT, which doesn't promise 'everything'. He just wants to hear again from responder without jumping.

1 mi – 2 mi– 2 Maj: 5-6 with 6 of the minor. Responder has no 4-card major.

1♣ - 2♣, forcing

2NT- Forcing to 3♣

> 3♣ - Non-forcing
>
> 3◊/3♡/3♠ - Singletons
>
> 3NT – To Play
>
> 4♣ - Keycard Blackwood for clubs

1◊ - 2◊, **forcing**

2NT – Forcing to 3◊

> 3◊ - Non-forcing
>
> 3♣ - Can be played as singleton or 5/5, (or both with more notes)
>
> 3♡/3♠ - Singleton
>
> 3NT – To Play
>
> 4◊ - Keycard Blackwood for diamonds

SPLINTER RAISES AFTER MINOR OPENINGS

Inverted raises should be limited to about twelve or so HCP. With extras and shortage, responder should splinter at first opportunity. This was discussed in the earlier chapter on splinters.

1♣ - 3◊/3♡/3♠ Shortness, big club raise, 12+ HCP

1◊ - 3♡/3♠ Shortness, big diamond raise, 12+ HCP

(1◊ - 3♣ is natural, 9-11, NF)

MAKING SLAM OR DOWN IN GAME

```
                    ♠ A K 4
                    ♡ A 4 3
                    ◇ 7 6 5 4
                    ♣ K 4 3
♠ J 10 5                              ♠ 9 8 7 6
♡ J 10 8 6 5                          ♡ K Q 9 7
◇ K 8                                 ◇ J 9
♣ 8 7 5                               ♣ 10 9 6
                    ♠ Q 3 2
                    ♡ 2
                    ◇ A Q 10 3 2
                    ♣ A Q J 2
```

South opened 1◇ and North bid 3NT since they were playing 2NT as invitational. South had no option other than to pass. East led a heart and North was quickly down after the diamond finesse lost.

How should this have been prevented? Consider this auction.

South	North	
1◇	2NT*	* Game forcing, no 4-card major
3♡^	3♠*	^ Singleton or void * Cue bid or fragment
3NT	4◇ ^	^ 3♠ was cue bid, unlikely to have first nine tricks
4♣	6◇	

Another example of the advantage of playing 2NT as forcing, to allow opener room to describe his hand.

Thanks to Anne Lund for this deal.

Shortness After 1NT Openings

The purpose of being able to show singletons after notrump openings is twofold. One is to stay out of notrump contracts when they are wrong, like Jxx opposite a singleton. The other is more constructive, often for slam purposes or just finding the best game. Of course, the question is should you?

Danny Kleinman points out, that as in the Monkees' hit song, Shades of Gray, a line says, [it was easy then to tell...] "the foolish from the wise." What's always been hard in bridge is to tell the clever from the wise.

There are clever ways to show singletons after notrump openings, but is it always wise to do so? Danny ventures to say, "Yes....when slam is in prospect and you can do so while preserving your prospects for stopping in the right game if you don't bid slam.....without diminishing your chances of success in the contracts you reach. Otherwise, no."

As Freddy Hamilton points out, you are giving the opponents a roadmap of what to lead. Left on their own, on a blind 1NT – 3NT auction, the odds favor the declarer's chance of success.

A treatment used by many partnerships is to play that after a 1NT opening, a jump to 3♡ or 3♠ shows shortness, most likely 1=3=4=5 (or 5=4) or 3=1=5=4 (or 4=5) distribution with game forcing values. For example:

Opener: ♠9753 ♡AJ9 ◇KJ ♣AQJ8

Responder ♠5 ♡KQ5 ◇AQ85 ♣109853

With no agreements, this is a 1NT – 3NT, good luck partner. But playing splinters, responder has a three-suited hand and is usually searching for the right game rather than slam. Subsequent cue bids of the short suit are the only slam tries, all other bids are natural. Let's take a look.

North	South		
1NT	3♣		
4♣^	4♠*	^ Not interested in notrump	* Slam interest
6♣			

All of opener's points are in responder's suits. After South's cue bid, North knows he must have the right hand for slam.

Let's see some more examples.

West	East	West	East
♠ K 4 2	♠ J 7 5	1NT	3♡* * Worried about hearts
♡ A K J	♡ 7	3NT^	^ Don't worry, be happy
◇ K J 9 5	◇ A Q 8 4		
♣ Q 9 4	♣ A J 7 6 2		

West	East	West	East
♠ A 6 4 2	♠ 7	1NT	3♠
♡ K Q J 10	♡ 9 7 3	4♡*	*Spade stopper but
◇ K 5	◇ A 9 7 4 2		suit oriented and happy
♣ K 5 2	♣ A J 9 6		to play the 4-3 fit

West	East	West	East
♠ K 7 6 4	♠ 9 5 2	1NT	3♥
♡ J 3 2	♡ 9	4♣^	5♣
◇ K Q	◇ A Q J 4		^ No interest in
♣ A K J 9	♣ Q 8 7 5 3		playing 3NT

You have ♠ void   ♡ K Q 5 2   ◇ A Q 8 5   ♣ 10 9 6 5 3

North	South
1NT	2♣ (please partner, bid 2♡)
2♠	3NT

While partner's spade response may have inhibited a spade lead, it's very annoying to watch the opponents take the first five tricks in spades when if partner was in, she had plenty of tricks. You might just bid 1NT – 3♠ with this hand too.

Many years ago when first filling out a convention card with Freddy, my partner for more years than I can remember, I suggested we play this. He was horrified, saying, "What, and tell them what to lead against 3NT?" But we have played this treatment ever since with much success.

MORE JUMPING OVER NOTRUMP

We know what 3♡/3♠ means after 1NT. What about 3♣/3◊? There are various treatments available. Some use 3♣ as Puppet Stayman. Let's focus on 3◊. This is a good way to handle 5/5 in the minors with game interest or more. Personally, I like 3♣ as 5/5 game only and 3◊ to be 5/5 slam interest.

The important thing if you have game interest only is the question of 3NT or not. You are known to have a singleton, unless you were dealt fourteen cards. Hey, it happens. If opener wants to know where your singleton is, he 'asks' in the usual manner- the next step.

If the auction has proceeded: North South\

                                    1NT   3◊* 5/5 Minors, strength unknown

                                    3♡^   ^ Where is your singleton?

We respond in the same fashion. There is no 'no' step since you are known to have one; you checked, only thirteen cards. The first step is the lowest suit, hearts. The second step is spades. DO NOT MEMORIZE THIS.

If your shape is 2=1=5=5, the response to the 3♡ ask is 3♠, heart shortage. If 1=2=5=5, bid 3NT, spade shortage. Note: If your hand is so strong you are afraid of being passed in 3NT, bid 4♣ instead.

For example: ♠K 3 ♡4 ◊A Q 7 5 3 ♣K Q 10 9 8 after partner opens 1NT, bid 3◊. When partner asks with 3♡, bid 3♠ showing heart shortage.

Opener will evaluate her hand. With heart wastage like ♡K J 5, opener will look for 3NT, otherwise will look for slam. Give opener:

  ♠A Q J ♡K J 5 ◊K 6 2 ♣J 7 5 3, opener will bid 3NT.

But with: ♠A Q J ♡J 8 6 3 ◊K 6 4 ♣A 5 3 will bid 4♣ looking for slam.

MORE SHORTNESS AFTER 1NT CONVENTIONS

There are several ways to show shortness after the common conventions including Stayman, Jacoby, and Texas. Let's take them one at a time. These are easy. Notice that you are 'telling' by jumping in your short suit.

STAYMAN:

1NT	2♣	
2♥	3♠	Slam try in hearts, may or may not be a singleton
	4♣	Slam try in hearts, singleton club (Please don't tell me Gerber)
	4♦	Slam try in hearts, singleton diamond

2♠	4♣	
	4♦	These are all singletons, slam tries in spades.
	4♥	

JACOBY TRANSFER

1NT	2♦	Jacoby Transfer to hearts
2♥	3♠	
	4♣	These jumps all show 6+ hearts, singleton in suits named
	4♦	and are slam tries in hearts

1NT	2♥*	Jacoby Transfer to spades
2♠	4♣	
	4♦	These jumps all show 6+ spades, singletons in the suits
	4♥	named and are slam tries in spades

Often players bid Texas with these hands, then 4NT Keycard, and have to sign off at the five level. Using Jacoby first and then showing shortness allows opener to express an opinion and may allow the bidding to stop at the four level.

Yes, there are more complicated systems to show voids versus singletons, but beyond the scope of this discussion. These treatments are available.

JACOBY OR TEXAS?

                            ♠ A Q J
                            ♡ K 8 7
                            ◇ Q 9 7
                            ♣ K J 3 2

        ♠ 7 5   ♠ 8 6
        ♡ Q 10 9   ♡ 6 5 4 3
        ◇ 10 8 6 5 4   ◇ A 2
        ♣ J 8 6   ♣ A Q 9 5 4

                            ♠ K 10 9 4 3 2
                            ♡ A J 2
                            ◇ K J 3
                            ♣ 7

North	South
1NT	2♡*	* Transfer to spades
2♠	4♣^	^ Splinter, club shortage with 6+ spades

(Please, STOP with the Gerber)

South has a good hand. He might have a cold slam if North has all working cards. Instead of bidding Texas, then making a Keycard ask, which commits the partnership to the 5-level, just transfer to 2♠ and splinter with 4♣ to describe your hand.

Do you think South, looking at ♣ KJ32 will be interested? Do you think the 5-level is safe?

SLAM ON AIR

♠ K 10 9 8 6 4
♡ K Q 7
◊ A 8 7
♣ 5

♠ J 5
♡ J 9 8 5
◊ 10 5
♣ A Q 9 8 6

♠ 3 2
♡ 10 6 4
◊ 9 4 2
♣ K J 9 7 2

♠ A Q 7
♡ A 3 2
◊ K Q J 6 3
♣ 4 3

South	North	
1NT	2♡*	* Transfer to spades
2♠	4♣^	^ Splinter raise of spades
4NT^	5♡*	^ Finally I think I have the right hand * 2 Keycards, no queen
6♠*	All Pass	* Thanks, just what the doctor ordered!

A very nice 34 point deck slam, sixteen opposite twelve. These are the ones that win tournaments.

OK, ONE FOR THE STAR STATE

                          ♠ A Q
                          ♡ A 8 6 2
                          ◇ A Q
                          ♣ A Q 9 8 3
    ♠ 9 5   ♠ 4 2
    ♡ J 9 5 3   ♡ Q 10 7 4
    ◇ 8 6 2   ◇ 10 9 7 3
    ♣ 10 7 4 2   ♣ K J 5
                          ♠ K J 10 8 7 6 3
                          ♡ K
                          ♣ K J 5 4
                          ◇ 6

North opens 2♣ and rebids 2NT. What would be your plan? Are you interested in a slam? Sure, but what's the best approach? Previously we used a Jacoby Transfer and a splinter raise to stay low.

We can't do that here. And if we could, which singleton? Here I would chance the five-level. Let's see how this auction works out:

North	South	
2♣	2◇	* Waiting
2NT	4♡*	* Texas transfer to spades, 6+ spades, strength unknown
4♠	4NT^	^ Keycard ask in spades
5♣*	5◇^	* 1 or 4, obviously 4 ^ Do you have the trump queen?
5♠^	7♠	* Yes, 2nd step, no kings

What do you need to make seven spades? You don't need any kings, but in the absence of any further queen asking bids, it's now or never.

If your partner has the heart queen, you have thirteen tricks. If she has the diamond queen, thirteen tricks. If she can ruff a diamond in hand, thirteen tricks. What do you think about your chances? Where are the rest of her HCP?

If you only bid 6♠, I think you win the "Wimp of the Week" award.

SHORTNESS AFTER MINOR SUIT TRANSFERS

Again the most common use of showing shortness in these situations is looking for the right game. Do we belong in 3NT or not? It's "I have a singleton. If I know that you know and you still want to be in 3NT, fine with me."

Without going into a detailed discussion, let's focus on the issue of shortness. After all, that's what this book is supposed to be about. I'll be glad to send you more details. Here is what I suggest you play.

1NT – 2♠ Clubs, any strength (Often played as strength asking)
2NT – I don't like clubs
or   then 3◊, 3♡, 3♠ Shortness, game forcing or stronger
3♣ - I do like clubs

1NT – 2NT Diamonds, any strength (To invite in notrump, bid 2♣, then 2NT)
3♣ - I don't like diamonds
or   then 3♡, 3♠ Shortness, game forcing or stronger
3◊ - I do like diamonds (who doesn't) (Short club- see complex notes)

But one can argue, is showing shortness the right way to go? Clever yes, but wise? Our goal is reaching the right contract, the right strain at the right level. With major suits, we can accomplish these tasks reasonable easily. We find an eight or nine card fit and go from these.

But with the minors, even a nine-card fit often doesn't suffice and there is less bidding room available to accomplish our task without losing 3NT as an option. In trying for five of a minor when 3NT is a possible contract, we are aiming at a very narrow target. Perhaps stoppers are more significant than shortness.

Concealment of weakness, strength, and shortness in other suits is an issue. In seeking certainty about stoppers, we may turn a 66% 3NT (leads in two of the other three suits will let us romp home with nine tricks, but in one of those suits an opening lead will beat us) into a 0% 3NT. As Danny says, "Achilles, don't go barefoot!"

For example with a 6-card minor but balanced, some 2326 and no slam interest, it's usually right to just raise 1NT to 3NT: ♠A2   ♥J86   ◆Q5   ◆KJ10543

NICE CATCH

```
                    ♠ 4
                    ♡ K 10 5
                    ◊ A K 3
                    ♣ Q J 9 7 4 3
   ♠ K 10 7 6                          ♠ Q 9 8 5 2
   ♡ 9 6 2                             ♡ A 8 4
   ◊ Q 10 7 6                          ◊ J 9 5
   ♣ 6 2                               ♣ 8 5
                    ♠ A J 3
                    ♡ Q J 7 3
                    ◊ 8 4 2
                    ♣ A K 10
```

South	West	North	East
1NT	P	2♣*	P	* Club, any strength
3♣^	P	3♠*	P	^ Likes clubs * Short spade
4♣	P	4◊	P	
4♠	P	6♣	All Pass	

South faced a difficult decision over North's 3♠ bid. Did he have enough high cards outside of his secondary spade values to make a progressive move past the safe haven of 3NT.

North was a bit aggressive at the end but caught the dummy he needed.

South could have had: ♠ A J 3 2 ♡ Q 7 3 ◊ J 8 4 ♣ A K 10 in which case 5♣ was the limit of the deal.

LOVE THOSE CUBBIES, I MEAN CLUBBIES.

```
              ♠ A 5 4
              ♡ K J 4
              ◇ K Q 8 5
              ♣ K 8 3
♠ K J 9 2                        ♠ Q 10 8 6 3
♡ Q 10 9 8                       ♡ 6 5 2
◇ J 7 4                          ◇ 10 6 2
♣ J 9                            ♣ 4 2
              ♠ 7
              ♡ A 7 3
              ◇ A 9 3
              ♣ A Q 10 7 6 5
```

North	East	South	West	
1NT	P	2♣*	P	* Clubs, any strength
3♣^	P	3♠*	P	^ Likes clubs * Short spade
4♣	P	4◇	P	
4♠	P	6♣	All Pass	

North certainly liked his hand for clubs. the ♠A opposite a singleton is fine, good trump support and lots of controls. 7♣ is not terrible; 3-3 diamonds or falling back then on a spade finesse.

I'm happy in 6♣. Someone will complain we are not in 6NT. Well, we are not playing matchpoints.

ALL THE MARBLES

```
              ♠ A 2
              ♡ A K 5 4
              ◊ 10 7 2
              ♣ A Q 10 4
♠ 9 8 7 5                        ♠ K 10 6 3
♡ 10 9 8                         ♡ J 7 6 3 2
◊ 8                              ◊ J 6
♣ J 9 5 3 2                      ♣ 8 7
              ♠ Q J 4
              ♡ Q
              ◊ A K Q 9 5 4 3
              ♣ K 6
```

North	East	South	West	
1NT	P	2NT*	P	* Diamonds, any strength
3◊^	P	3♡*	P	^ Likes diamonds * Shortness
3NT	P	4◊^	P	^ Slam interest
4♡	P	5♣	P	
5♠	P	7◊	All Pass	

Shortness is often the key as we have discussed. South showed his singleton heart and North with heart wastage signed off. But South had too much in the way of extra values.

After North's two cue bids, South with a solid suit bid what he thought he could make.

OVERBOARD

```
                    ♠ K 8
                    ♡ A Q J 10 6 4
                    ◊ K J 10 7
                    ♣ 4
   ♠ 10 5 4                              ♣ A 9 6 2
   ♡ 9 5 2                               ♡ K
   ◊ 2                                   ◊ 9 8 6 3
   ♣ J 9 8 6 3 2                         ♣ Q 10 7 5
                    ♠ Q J 7 3
                    ♡ 8 7 3
                    ◊ A Q 5 4
                    ♣ A K
```

South	West	North	East	
1NT	P	4◊*	P	* Texas transfer to hearts
4♡	P	4♠^	P	^ Kickback Keycard Blackwood for hearts
5◊*	P	5♡	All Pass	* Two Keycards, no queen of trump

West led the ◊ 2.

Notice the irony in this hand. Declarer wins the opening lead and starts the trumps. If he takes a finesse, East will win and give West a diamond ruff. Then back to East's spade ace for another diamond ruff. Down two.

But if South decides to forego the trump finesse and go up ace, he makes an overtrick.

You will recall we discussed earlier that perhaps a better way to bid this hand and get partner involved would be this auction:

South	North	
1NT	2◊*	* Jacoby transfer to hearts
2♡	4♣^	* Singleton club, heart slam try
4♡*	All Pass	* Not interested, club wastage, bad hearts

North-South would be at a safer level. When both partners are involved in decision making, results are usually better.

Shortness After Opening 2NT

Besides your usual Stayman and Jacoby, for 1-suited minor slam tries, a simple way is use Stayman followed by four of the minor, natural and slammish. You may not have a 4-card major. 4NT by opener is always an attempt to sign-off, any other bid is positive.

> For example: 2NT - 3♣
>
>   any bid – 4 of a minor is natural and slammish
>   4NT- To Play, no slam interest

OK, straight forward, STOP here. Read further only at your own risk. As you see on the TV commercials, "For professional drivers only."

If you want to play a little more complex to show more shape and shortness, a little fancy footwork is necessary. It's really easy, but you will forget and mess it up a few times. That's OK, everybody does. Just understand that after 2NT, or 2♣ then 2NT, that EVERYTHING, except Stayman, is a transfer.

You already play that 3◊>3♡ and 3♡>3♠, so just keep it going;

3♠>3NT, 3NT>4♣, and 4♣>4◊. This means the only way to 3NT after 2NT is to bid 3♠, a small price to pay for a big payout. But of course. everyone forgets the first few times and the bidding goes a casual 2NT-3NT. Now what?

2NT	3♠*	* Forces 3NT	
3NT	P	Only way to play 3NT	
	4♣	2=1=5=5	All bidding is then natural
	4◊	1=2=5=5	
	4♡	3=1=4=5 or 5=4	
	4♠	1=3=4=5 or 5=4	
	4NT	2=2=4=5 or 5=4 non-forcing	

OK, so far pretty much all the same.

But here comes the big difference: The minor suit transfers. See next page.

2NT 3NT* * Forces 4♣, a single suit club slam try
4♣   4◊
            4♡ are all singletons, just like we play after 1NT-2♠
            4♠
            4NT Quantitative, non-forcing, no singletons
4NT by opener is to play, not interested

2NT 4♣ * Forces 4◊, Same with one-suiter in diamonds
4◊   4♡
            4♠ are singletons
            4NT quantitative, no singletons
4NT by opener to play, not interested

**** So what can opener do if she is interested in a slam after the transfer and the singleton. 4NT is a sign-off; Opener has to have a 'no thanks' bid.

If opener is interested, treat responders bid, the singleton, as a Keycard ask.
Let's see.
2NT   4♣
4◊   4♡ (Singleton)
OK, I'm interested. I'm treating 4♡ as Keycard Blackwood. I have three keycards and we play 1430. 4♠ is the first step, 4NT is the second step but that's my sign-off bid so the second step must be 5♣.
5♣   6◊
All Pass

SPLINTERS OVER 2NT

```
                        ♠ A K 7 3
                        ♡ A 2
                        ◇ A 9 8 4
                        ♣ K Q 3
        ♠ 10 4                              ♠ 9 8 6 5
        ♡ K J 8 6 4                         ♡ Q 10 9 7 5
        ◇ 6 2                               ◇ J 5
        ♣ 8 6 5 2                           ♣ A 7
                        ♠ Q J 2
                        ♡ 3
                        ◇ K Q 10 7 3
                        ♣ J 10 9 4
```

North	South
2NT	3♠^	^ Transfer to 3NT
3NT	4♡ *	* 3=1=4=5 (5=4)
5◇	6◇	
All Pass		

Here is a typical hand that might be bid 2NT – 4NT or more, going down in notrump with a normal heart lead.

Playing splinters, an easy 6◇ contract is reached.

ANOTHER SPLINTER OVER 2NT

```
                    ♠ 10
                    ♡ A Q 8
                    ◊ K J 10 7 2
                    ♣ J 10 5 3
♠ K J 6 2                              ♠ 9 7 5 4 3
♡ 9 7 2                               ♡ 6 5 3
◊ A 9 3                               ◊ 8 6 5
♣ 9 7 4                               ♣ 8 6
                    ♠ A Q 8
                    ♡ K J 10 4
                    ◊ Q 4
                    ♣ A K Q 2
```

South	North	
2NT	3♠*	* Transfer to 3NT
3NT	4♠*	* 1=3=4=5 (5=4)
6♣		
	All pass	

This time the 2NT opener has partner's shortness covered. Opener is very happy to play in a minor slam. If opener didn't like the minors, he would bid 4NT, a sigh-off bid.

3NT followed by 4NT is always to play. Opener needs a 'no' bid.

Shortness Is Not Always Good News

So far we have been discussing the value of shortness in game and slam bidding, in staying out of 3NT when necessary, etc. Let me show you a common situation where a singleton causes you more headaches than I could prescribe medication for. I'm talking about the hands with a singleton spade.

You are dealer and have ♠7 ♡A84 ◊Q853 ♣AK1052

What's the problem you ask? Nothing yet, hang on. You open 1♣ and of course partner bids 1♠. I have never had a partner bid 1♡ so I could bid 2♡. But enough about me. What are you going to choose for a rebid after 1♠?

What are your choices? 1NT? 2♣? Maybe you want to go back and open 1◊ so now you can bid 2♣? Jerry Helms wrote an excellent paper on this topic some years ago. Here are some of his thoughts and mine.

If you rebid 2♣, partner will assume you have a six-card suit. With ♣Qx, she might visualize six club tricks and bid 2NT with some 5-3-3-2 eleven count, certainly a precarious contract. Had you rebid 1NT, she would likely pass.

If you take a mulligan and try the 1◊ - 2♣ approach, you would probably find yourself in the same precarious 2NT or even 3◊ after partner makes a jump preference. Of course, if partner has a weak hand with three clubs and one diamond, she will leave you in 2♣. However, the real disaster comes when partner has a weak hand with 3-3 or 2-2 in the minors and takes the mandatory 2◊ preference.

If you must risk playing in two of a suit with a 4-2 fit, do so only with a strong 4-card suit like ♠7 ♡A84 ◊AK105 ♣Q8532. Now 1◊ -1♠; 2♣ is fine.

What about a 1NT rebid? If partner has some 6-3-2-2 thirteen count, she will bid 4♠. 3NT is a much better contract, easier to reach with the other auctions.

OK, so what's it going to be? Ask different experts and you will get different answers. That's what makes horse racing. So which horse are you riding off on?

I like the 1NT rebid because it defines my HCP, keeps the bidding low, and doesn't suggest a source of tricks.

My second choice is rebidding 2♣ - at least it limits your strength, and you have a chance of staying low. Of course, you have lost 1NT if it was right.

The least appealing horse is 1◊ - 2♣. You can't get to 1NT if it was right, you haven't defined your HCP which could be 12-18, and you often get a preference to your 4-card suit. And you may miss a big heart fit.

Try this deal: ♠4 ♡A Q 7 6 ◊A J 9 7 5 ♣Q 8 3

You open 1◊ and partner bids 1NT. The opponents are silent. What is your call? What are your choices? Pass? 2◊? Other?

This was a hand from the It's Your Call in the ACBL Bulletin some time ago. Want to match your answer against the expert panel? What have you come up with?

Did you pass? Of the nineteen panelists, two passed and two bid 2◊. The other fifteen bid 2♣, figuring they would hit partner in one minor or another.

Comments included "Seems obvious," "Easy," "Partner doesn't have more than three spades and I want to play in a suit," "The opponents' 2♠ balance is coming if we pass 1NT," "We have an eight-card minor fit somewhere. Bidding 2♣ will find it."

Here is a similar problem.   ♠9 ♡Q J 7 2 ◊A 6 5 4 3 ♣K Q 3

After South opens 1◊ and North bids 1♠, what are South's rebid options?
1NT, 2◊, 2♡, or other? Passing is out, 1NT with a singleton is not appealing,
2◊ with that suit doesn't seem right, and 2♡ would be a reverse showing a 19+ point hand. Great! So by process of elimination, we are left with_____2♣.
Really, a 3-card suit? Why not, we open or bid 3-card suits often. If partner has a minimum with equal minor suit length, she will bid 2◊. If she passes, it's probably your best spot.

How about   ♠10 ♡A J 5 3 ◊K J 8 4 ♣A Q 5 3

While I much prefer opening 1♣ with 4-4 in the minors you need to plan ahead with distributional hands, especially spade shortness. You open 1◊ and partner bids 1♠ (of course). Rebid 2♣, not 1NT. Partner will know you have at least eight, probably nine cards in the minors and are unbalanced since you didn't bid 1NT. He persists with 2♠. Now what? 2NT? You have 15 HCP.

No, this deal is a misfit and you should want out as fast as possible. Partner knows you likely have a singleton spade and she rebid them anyway.

Would you open in first seat with ♠ 2   ♡ J 10 5 3   ◊ A Q 7 4   ♣ K J 7 3

Whenever you have spade shortness, anticipate problems. A minimum hand, hard pressed for a rebid, I would pass.

Note however, that a permutation of suits, will make this a fine 1♣ opening. Rearrange to ♠ K J 7 3   ♡ 2   ◊ J 10 5 3   ♣ K J 7 3, still a marginal eleven point hand but can be opened more freely.

Bidding manuals incorrectly instruct players to ask themselves "Should I open?" as Step 1, and then "Which suit should I open?" as Step 2. A better procedure is "Step 1, if I open, what will I open and what will I rebid over partner's most awkward new-suit response?" Then "Step 2. Is the plan of Step 1 better than passing?"

There is life after pass.

Doubling Splinter Bids

You are sitting quietly with your meager collection of a few good cards while the opponents are busy bidding away. The player on your right makes a splinter bid, showing shortness and trump support. You have the ace of that suit, or some other good holding and partner is going to be on lead. Should you double and if you do, what should it mean?

Doubling a splinter bid for the lead of that suit is nonproductive for several reasons. It does little for you in the way of establishing tricks. It's often a trick you were going to score anyhow.

And a serious drawback is it gives the opponents room for an extra bid. They can pass and give your RHO an opportunity to make another bid, perhaps now a cue bid. Or an opponent may redouble to show a control.

So what should you do? Nothing? Of course not. I'm glad you asked. There are two types of splinters. First let's consider the one-suited splinter, an auction such as 1♠ -P – 4◊. Since we have agreed doubling for a diamond lead is silly, here is a treatment in use by many expert pairs. Put your double to better use.

Double asks for the lead of the higher unbid suit, in this case hearts. Passing means either you have no preference, or you prefer a club lead. But you definitely do not want a heart lead. My old teacher, a baseball fan, called this "designated hitter', DH, double for higher. It made it easy to remember.

What about the 2-suited splinter? An auction such as 1♣ -P - 1♠ - P

$$4♡ - ?$$

Your partner will be on lead against a spade contract. The agreement here should be double says "I can't stand the lead of the 4th suit," in this case diamonds. Pass says it's OK to lead a diamond or whatever you like.

Let's look at some example deals.

TO DOUBLE OR NOT TO DOUBLE

```
                    ♠ Q 6 5 4
                    ♡ 9 4
                    ◊ 6 3
                    ♣ 10 8 7 4 2
      ♠ A 7 3                            ♠ J 8 2
      ♡ A J 8 5 3                        ♡ K Q 7 6 2
      ◊ J 7 2                            ◊ A K 8 4
      ♣ K 3                              ♣ 9
                    ♠ K 10 9
                    ♡ 10
                    ◊ Q 10 9 5
                    ♣ A Q J 6 5
```

West	North	East	South
1♡	P	4♣	Dbl* * No agreements
4♡	All Pass		

West asked North if they had any agreement about South's double. North said no. East-West reached 4♡ and North led the ♣ 4.

South won the opening lead and shifted to a spade. Declarer discarded one of dummy's spade losers on the club king. He made four hearts, losing one trick in each suit except trump.

Was there a more successful lead?

A trump lead gives declarer time to set up a club or diamond for a spade discard.
A club lead set up declarer's king for a spade discard.
A diamond lead gives declarer time to set up a diamond for a spade discard.

So had North-South been playing "Designated Hitter" South's double would call for the higher suit, spades.

Down one.

DESIGNATED HITTER

```
                    ♠ Q J 8 3
                    ♡ Q 9 8 3
                    ◇ K Q 8 2
                    ♣ 5
        ♠ K 7 6                         ♠ A 9 5 2
        ♡ 6 5 2                         ♡ void
        ◇ 5 4                           ◇ J 10 9 7 6 3
        ♣ J 10 9 8 4                    ♣ 6 3 2
                    ♠ 10 4
                    ♡ A K J 10 7 4
                    ◇ A
                    ♣ A K Q 7
```

South	West	North	East	
2♣	P	2◇*	P	* Waiting
2♡	P	4♣^	P	^ Splinter, club shortness with hearts
6♡	All Pass			

West led the ♣ J.

South's jump to slam wasn't terrible, leaving West with less information for his opening lead. After the club lead, the slam was cold.

What could the defense have done?

Playing lead directing doubles of splinters to be meaningful, if East had doubled 4♣, that would have suggested the lead of the higher of the other two suits, spades.

Perhaps West should have led a spade anyhow, easy to say now.

SPLINTER DOUBLES

```
                      ♠ K Q J 5
                      ♡ Q J 10 4
                      ◊ 6
                      ♣ A 10 3 2
    ♠ 4 3                                   ♠ 10 9 8
    ♡ K 8 7 5                               ♡ A 3
    ◊ A J 8 2                               ◊ K Q 10 7 5
    ♣ 8 5 4                                 ♣ 9 7 6
                      ♠ A 7 6 2
                      ♡ 9 6 2
                      ◊ 9 4 3
                      ♣ K Q J
```

North	East	South	West
1♣	P	1♠	P
3◊*	P^	4♠	All Pass

* Splinter, short diamond, 4 spades

^ I can stand the lead of the unbid suit

South liked his hand, three little diamonds opposite partner's shortness, so he bid game. East's pass said a heart lead was fine. He would have doubled the splinter if he could not stand a heart lead.

West led a heart. East won and returned a heart West gave East a heart ruff. The diamond ace was the setting trick.

Would West have led a heart anyhow?

Lead Your Singleton? Yes or No?

You are on lead against a suit contract and you have a singleton. Should you lead it? Maybe. You need ask yourself "Self, can I likely get partner on lead to give me a ruff, and will I have any trumps in my hand by that time?"

Of course, if partner holds the ace of your short suit, no problem. But otherwise, there may be a lot of work to do. If partner bid the suit, that's a strong candidate for your singleton opening lead.

Suppose you hold the AKx in a different suit and lead the ace first to 'get a look'. If you then lead your singleton, partner is likely to return your first suit. The many-time world champion Benito Garozzo is famously often quoted as "if you don't lead one, you don't have one." Your partner is far more likely to recognize a singleton at Trick 1 than later in the hand.

What about a singleton in a suit bid by the opponents? This is far less clear than when partner bid the suit. They are likely to hold several cards in that suit, a suit they are going to want to develop. Your lead is far more likely to do more harm for you than good.

Holding a control in the trump suit is a key factor to be considered. If partner can't win Trick 1 and give you an immediate ruff, at least you are likely to be regaining the lead and will have a second chance. If you have a likely natural trump trick, a holding like QJx, it's probably best to look for a different lead.

Also, when you (or you know you partner has) trump length, four or more, leading from length to shorten declarer is usually best, a forcing defense.

Let's look at some examples.

West	North	East	South (You)
1♣	1♡	1♠	2♡
2♠	3♡	4♠	All Pass

1) ♠973 ♡K642 ◊KJ763 ♣5

2) ♠J865 ♡K42 ◊KJ763 ♣5

3) ♠A86 ♡K842 ◊J9763 ♣5

1) Lead the ♡ 2. Likely declarer will be drawing trumps and running clubs. A club lead will only make life easier for him. You want to try to establish a heart winner while you can,

2) Lead the ♡ 2. With trump length, you hope dummy has three or four hearts and you can force declarer to ruff, shortening his trump holding. You hope to score your red suit winners in the end.

3) Lead the ♣ 5. With trump control, the ace, you have a reasonable chance to get partner on lead with a heart later, a perfect time for a singleton lead.

East	South (You)	West	North
1NT	P	2♣	P
2♡	P	4♡	All Pass

4) ♠8753 ♡KQ7 ◊AQJ86 ♣J

4) Lead a spade. Yes, you have a trump entry and a singleton. But with so much strength, your partner is broke or nearly broke. A club lead may pickle partner's possible club trick (partner might have ♣Q952). You should not seek a ruff anyhow as it may come at the expense of a trump trick. Make a passive lead, hoping to take your tricks.

West	North	East	South (You)
1♠	2◊	2♡	3◊
3♡	P	4♡	All Pass

5) ♠7 ♡963 ◊KQ973 ♣Q964

6) ♠7 ♡A75 ◊9873 ♣K10964

5) Lead the ◊ King. You can't hope for more than one diamond trick and it could go away. Spade tricks are not going anywhere. If dummy comes down with diamond shortness, you can switch. Leading the singleton spade is wishful thinking.

6) Here you might try the ♠7 and hope to get a diamond, a spade, a heart, and another trick? On a good day, partner has some aces.

What about against a small slam? Do not lead a singleton if you have an ace. Partner can't have the ace you need and you will probably be helping declarer.

On the other hand, if you don't have an ace, a singleton lead has a much better chance of succeeding. With a little luck, partner will have the ace of your suit or the ace of trumps.

What about leading a singleton trump? Since this is so rarely right, if you never did this, you would probably be far ahead in the game. If you have only one, likely your partner has some length, not a lot.

More often than not, you will take away declarer's problem in the suit. When to lead trumps is a discussion for another day.

CHOICE OF LEADS

$$\spadesuit\ K\ 9\ 6$$
$$\heartsuit\ K\ 10\ 4\ 3$$
$$\diamond\ 6\ 2$$
$$\clubsuit\ 7\ 5\ 4\ 2$$

♠ A J 4 3	♠ 7
♡ 5	♡ Q 9 8 6 2
◊ Q 9 5	◊ J 8 7 4 3
♣ K J 10 9 3	♣ A 8

$$\spadesuit\ Q\ 10\ 8\ 5\ 2$$
$$\heartsuit\ A\ J\ 7$$
$$\diamond\ A\ K\ 10$$
$$\clubsuit\ Q\ 6$$

South opened 1♠. North raised to 2♠, ending the auction. West led the ♡ 5

Declarer won the opening lead, played a spade to the king, cashed the ◊AK and ruffed a diamond. He played a second spade. The defense took two club tricks, and West won three trump tricks, but declarer was in control.

Making two spades.

How would declarer have done with a club lead, a forcing defense?

When you have long trumps, do not be so quick to lead a singleton. If you lead your long suit, clubs, East wins and returns the suit. West continues clubs forcing declarer to ruff.

He leads a spade to the king and plays three rounds of diamonds, ruffing the third.

Now he leads a trump. West wins two rounds of spades and leads another club. This leaves West with a winning spade and a winning club. Declarer is down one.

You expected to get trump tricks, but you were able to make declarer ruff and you gained control.

It's A Singleton; Win or Duck?

There are many reasons why a defender in second seat may have to play high to a trick. Danny and I wrote a whole book on this subject. But there are unusual exceptions where it seems obvious to play high and of course it's wrong.

Here is the most common:

Dummy has singleton 9

East (You) A 6 4 2

Should you play your ace on air when declarer leads dummy's singleton?

Drumroll please: "yes, no and maybe!"

Yes, if this will be the setting trick, you should probably take it.

Otherwise, probably no, though of course we should see the other suits, the auction, and the previous play to be confident.

Let's see why. Suppose this is the layout:

```
                9
  Q 10 6 4 3              A 7 5 2
              K J 8
```

If you play low, declarer must guess. He may play the jack, thinking you would always play the ace if you had it. This assumes that you duck smoothly. Be ready to play in normal tempo.

Here is another position, a singleton from the dummy:

```
                3
   J 10 6 4               A 9 7 2
              K Q 8 5
```

Or a singleton towards the dummy:

```
              K Q 8 5
   A 9 7 2               J 10 6 4
                3
```

113

In both cases, ducking sacrifices one fast trick to get two slow tricks

Here is another common lay-out:

                            3
    K 8 6 2   A 9 7 5
              Q J 10 4

In a suit contract, declarer may be planning a ruffing finesse. Who should win the first trick for the defense? Yes, the defender whose honor lies in front of, not behind, the hand with the sequence of honors.

Here that is West with the king. So when declarer leads the singleton, East must duck to allow West to win the king first, the honor that can be ruff-finessed.

Have you noticed that except for the setting trick, ducking is almost always right. Yet what do we usually see at the table? Yes, ace-risers.

Except they never seem to do it when I'm the declarer.

Mike Lawrence says "More than 90% of defenders would take their ace and 90% would be wrong....this is one of the hardest defensive plays....but it's a common play and often critical."

Danny Kleinman told me he is in a race with Eddie Kantar for the dubious honor of "Most Aces Lost by Ducking, Lifetime."

Let's look at some deals.

HIGH OR LOW?

```
                        ♠ 8
                        ♡ Q J 5 4 3
                        ◇ Q 8 7 5
                        ♣ Q 8 6
        ♠ 10 3                             ♠ A J 7 4 2
        ♡ 9 7                              ♡ A 6
        ◇ A J 10 6 4                       ◇ K 2
        ♣ J 7 5 3                          ♣ K 9 4 2
                        ♠ K Q 9 6 5
                        ♡ K 10 8 2
                        ◇ 9 3
                        ♣ A 10
```

South	West	North	East
1 ♠	P	1 NT*	P	* Forcing one round
2 ♡	P	3 ♡	All Pass

Opening Lead: ♡ 7

East won and returned a trump, won in dummy. Declarer led the singleton spade, East won the ace. Declarer had two high spades, four heart tricks in dummy, one club trick, and two ruffs in hand.

Nine tricks.

How can the defense prevail?

Say play starts the same, but when declarer leads the singleton spade, East ducks and declarer wins in hand. Declarer finishes with one high spade, four heart tricks in dummy, one club trick, and two ruffs in hand.

Eight tricks. Hmmm.

A SINGLETON IN THE DUMMY

♠ A J 10 7 6
♡ J 10
♢ 5
♣ Q J 7 6 5

♠ K 9 3 2   ♠ Q 8 4
♡ 6 3 2   ♡ 8 4
♢ Q 6   ♢ A 9 4 3 2
♣ K 10 8 3   ♣ 9 4 2

♠ 5
♡ A K Q 9 7 5
♢ K J 10 8 7
♣ A

South opened 1♡, then bid and rebid diamonds. When North showed a preference for hearts, South checked for Keycards and bid 6♡.

West led the ♣ 3.

Declarer won the opening lead and led a spade to the ace. He next led the singleton diamond from dummy, East played the ace.

After drawing trumps, declarer had the rest.

Could the defenders have done better?

Maybe. Play starts the same but when declarer leads the diamond, East should play low smoothly. Declarer will likely play the jack and West will win the queen. With not enough trumps to ruff out the diamond ace, declarer is down one.

Even if declarer guesses to play the king, East will score his ace at the end to break even.

SECOND HAND LOW

                    ♠ 7 6 3
                    ♡ Q 10 3
                    ♦ A Q 5
                    ♣ K Q 10 5

♠ Q J 10 2   ♠ K 9 8
♡ 8 4   ♡ 7 2
♦ 10 9 7   ♦ K J 4 2
♣ A 8 7 4   ♣ J 9 3 2

                    ♠ A 5 4
                    ♡ A K J 9 6 5
                    ♦ 8 6 3
                    ♣ 6

North   East   South   West
1 ♣   P   1 ♡   P
1 NT   P   4 ♡   All Pass

Opening Lead: ♠ Queen

Declarer won the opening lead and drew trumps. Then he led a club. West played the ace. The defense cashed two spade tricks, but declarer discarded his losing diamonds on the ♣ K-Q. Making four hearts.

How can the defense prevail?

Play starts the same until declarer leads his club. West must duck, essentially trading one trick to get two. West has to assume his partner has the ♦ K J to have a chance of defeating the contract.

By ducking the club, he loses his club trick, but gains two tricks. Declarer has to lose two diamonds and two spades.

Such positions are common. Unless it's the setting trick or a vital reason to be on lead, it's usually a good trade.

JUMP OR DUCK?

```
                    ♠ K Q J 8 6 3
                    ♡ 7
                    ♦ K 6 2
                    ♣ A 5 2
♠ 7                                    ♠ 4
♡ J 9 6 3 2                            ♡ A 10 8 5
♦ Q J 10 9                            ♦ 8 5 4 3
♣ K 8 4                               ♣ Q J 10 9
                    ♠ A 10 9 5 2
                    ♡ K Q 4
                    ♦ A 7
                    ♣ 7 6 3
```

South opened 1♠. North considered a 4♡ splinter but that would take up a lot of bidding space and he felt his hand was too strong. He bid 2NT, an artificial forcing raise (Jacoby).

When South signed off in 4♠, North checked for Keycards and bid 6♠.

West led the ◊ Queen.

Declarer won the opening lead and drew trumps. He led the singleton heart from dummy, East won the ace. Declarer claimed, discarding the two club losers on the two high hearts in hand.

Could the defenders defeat the slam?

A club lead would have defeated the contract by two tricks. However, when declarer leads the singleton heart from dummy, East must play low.

Now the slam cannot be made Declarer has no heart loser, but has the two club losers. Down one.

Courage!

A GOOD TRADE

```
                    ♠ 7 4 3
                    ♡ K 5 3
                    ◇ K Q 9 6
                    ♣ 9 4 3
     ♠ Q J 10 9                        ♠ K 8 6
     ♡ 7 2                             ♡ J 8
     ◇ A 7 5 4 3                       ◇ J 10 2
     ♣ Q 6                             ♣ K J 10 7 5
                    ♠ A 5 2
                    ♡ A Q 10 9 6 4
                    ◇ 8
                    ♣ A 8 2
```

South	West	North	East
1 ♡	P	2 ♡	P
4 ♡		All Pass	

Opening Lead: ♠ Queen

Declarer won the opening lead and led the eight of diamonds. West won the ace and cashed two spade tricks. Declarer won the club switch and drew trumps.

He discarded his two club losers on the two good diamonds in dummy.

Making four hearts.

How might the defense prevail?

When the declarer leads his singleton, West plays low, hopefully trading one trick for two. He won't take any diamond tricks, but the defense will take two clubs and two spades. A good trade.

Down one.

SWITCH TO YOUR SINGLETON?

♠ K Q J 9 4
♡ K Q 4
◇ A 7 4
♣ 4 2

East
♠ 2
♡ 7 6 2
◇ K J 5 3
♣ A 9 8 7 5

South	West	North	East
2♡	P	2NT	P
3♣*	P	4♡	All Pass

* Feature, ace or king

The opponents arrive in 4♡ on the above auction and partner leads the ♣ Q.
East wins the ace. How should he continue?

For sure on this auction partner, West, has the spade ace. What is his best hope to defeat 4♠? Should he return his singleton and obtain a spade ruff? Decide before looking on.

If you lead a spade and get a ruff, you won't get any more tricks. Declarer will then have six hearts, three spades, one diamond and one club trick.

Better to lead a diamond before setting up declarer's spades. If partner has the diamond queen, you may be able to set up two diamond tricks before declarer sets up the spades.

West
♠ A 8 7 6 5
♡ 9
◇ Q 9 6
♣ Q J 10 3

South
♠ 10 3
♡ A J 10 8 5 3
◇ 10 8 2
♣ K 6

SMOOTH

```
              ♠ K Q J 4
              ♡ 9 7 3
              ◊ 9
              ♣ A K Q 8 4
♠ 8 5                          ♠ 9 7 6
♡ Q J 10 6 4                   ♡ K 8 5
◊ Q 10 5 2                     ◊ A 8 3
♣ 9 7                          ♣ 10 6 5 3
              ♠ A 10 3 2
              ♡ A 2
              ◊ K J 7 6 4
              ♣ J 2
```

North opened 1♣ and South bid 1♠. North had to choose- 3◊? 4◊?

He bid 4◊. South should not have liked his hand but since he had a little extra, cue bid 4♡. North drove to 6♠. West led the ♡ Queen.

East played an encouraging eight at Trick 1 as declarer won the ace. Declarer drew trumps and played five rounds of clubs, discarding one heart and two diamonds from his hand.

He then led the diamond nine from the board and East won the ace. Declarer had the rest.

How might the defense have prevailed?

The first nine tricks are likely the same, but when declarer leads the diamond nine, East must duck smoothly. Declarer will likely play the diamond jack. He will end up losing two diamond tricks. Down one.

If declarer has ♦ K Q J remaining, nothing matters. The only hope to defeat the contract is for East to duck (smoothly) and hope declarer has to guess.

LOW AGAIN

$$\spadesuit K\,9\,6\,5\,2$$
$$\heartsuit 8\,5\,3$$
$$\diamond K\,Q\,5\,4$$
$$\clubsuit 5$$

$$\spadesuit 7\,3 \qquad\qquad \spadesuit 8\,4$$
$$\heartsuit Q\,9\,4\,2 \qquad\qquad \heartsuit K\,J\,10$$
$$\diamond 10\,8\,3 \qquad\qquad \diamond A\,J\,9$$
$$\clubsuit J\,10\,8\,4 \qquad\qquad \clubsuit A\,9\,7\,3\,2$$

$$\spadesuit A\,Q\,J\,10$$
$$\heartsuit A\,7\,6$$
$$\diamond 7\,6\,2$$
$$\clubsuit K\,Q\,6$$

East	South	West	North	
1♣	1NT	P	2♡*	* Spades
P	2♠	P	3♠	
P	4♠	All Pass		

Opening Lead: ♣ Jack

East won the ace and shifted to the heart jack. Declarer won, drew trumps, and discarded dummy's last two hearts on the K-Q of clubs. He later lost two diamonds, making four spades.

Was East too much of a rule follower?

Yes, we have seen this before. It's the same principle of dummy having something like K-Q x and declarer leads what you suspect is a singleton. Win, they take two. Duck, they take one.

If East ducks the opening lead, declarer is deprived of two discards. He must lose two hearts and two diamonds.

Down one.

BETTER GO LOW

```
              ♠ 9
              ♡ K J 5
              ◊ Q 9 6 3 2
              ♣ 10 8 7 4
♠ Q 6 2                        ♠ A 10 7 4
♡ 8 7 4                        ♡ 6 2
◊ K 8 5 4                      ◊ A 10 7
♣ 9 5 2                        ♣ Q J 6 3
              ♠ K J 8 5 3
              ◊ A Q 10 9 3
              ♦ J
              ♣ A K
```

South opened 1♠, North bid 1NT, forcing for one round. When South bid 2♡, North made a 'courtesy' raise. South bid 4♡. West led the ♡ 4.

Declarer won the opening lead in dummy and led a spade. East won the ace and played another trump. Declarer was able to set up his spade side suit easily with one ruff.

Making four hearts.

Could the defense do better?

After the same good opening lead, when declarer leads the spade from dummy. East must play low (smoothly please). Declarer will play the jack. West will win the queen and play another trump.

Declarer can't prevent East from later scoring two more spade tricks and one diamond trick. Even if declarer guesses spades correctly, one trick will be coming back.

WIN OR DUCK

```
            North
            ♠ Q 4          South        North
            ♡ A J 3        1♠           1NT* Forcing one round
            ◊ K J 8 7 3    2♡           2NT
   West     ♣ 9 7 5        3♠           4♠
   ♠ K 8                                All Pass
   ♡ 8 5 2
   ◊ A 10 6
   ♣ K 8 6 4 3
```

North-South reach 4♠ on the auction shown above. West leads the ♣ 4.

East plays the club queen at Trick 1 and declarer wins the ace. At Trick 2, declarer leads the diamond four. Do you win or duck? Why? Decide now.

Count your tricks. Count declarer's tricks. What's declarer's distribution?

From the bidding, he is likely 6-4 in the majors. He is known to have the club jack; partner played the queen at Trick 1. So his shape is 6=4=1=2. It appears declarer has ten tricks: five spades, probably three hearts, one diamond and the club ace.

Are your chances hopeless? Your tricks are the trump king, the club king, and the diamond ace. You have to hope partner can take a heart trick.

If you duck the diamond and declarer guesses to play the king, he makes his contract. Grab your ace, cash the club king, and exit a club and wait.

```
                              ♠ 7 3 2
                              ♡ Q 10 6
                              ◊ Q 9 5 2
                 South        ♣ Q 10 2
                 ♠ A J 10 9 6 5
                 ♡ K 9 7 4
                 ◊ 4
                 ♣ A J
```

With passive defense, partner will eventually win a heart trick for the setting trick. Did you think I was going to have you ducking on every deal?

ANOTHER GOOD TRADE

```
                    ♠ K Q 7 5
                    ♡ K 8 3
                    ♢ J 7 2
                    ♣ A J 6
   ♠ A 10 8 4                      ♠ J 6 3 2
   ♡ 6 5                           ♡ 10 7
   ♢ 10 9 3                        ♢ A K 6 5
   ♣ Q 9 4 3                       ♣ K 10 8
                    ♠ 9
                    ♡ A Q J 9 4 2
                    ♢ Q 8 4
                    ♣ 7 5 2
```

North opened 1♣ and South bid 1♡. North rebid 1NT. South's 4♡ bid was a stretch. West led the ♢10

East cashed the A-K of diamonds and played a third diamond. Declarer won and led a spade. West won the ace and shifted to a club. Declarer won the club ace, drew trumps, and discarded two clubs on the ♠ K Q.

Making four hearts.

Was there a better line of defense to defeat four hearts?

West can make a two-for-one trade. By ducking the spade, he gets two tricks in return. After declarer wins the spade king, he has to face the clubs. There is no way to avoid losing two club tricks.

East could have shifted to a club at Trick 3, but as long as West ducks the spade, four hearts is going down.

A good trade.

Printed in the United States
by Baker & Taylor Publisher Services

Printed in the United States
by Baker & Taylor Publisher Services